BY THE
GRACE *of* GOD

COMPILED BY BOB JONES III

Bob Jones University Press
Greenville, South Carolina 29614

By the Grace of God

Compiled by Bob Jones III

© 1996, 2000 Bob Jones University Press
Greenville, SC 29614

Printed in the United States of America
All rights reserved.

ISBN 0-89084-895-5

15   14   13   12   11   10   9   8   7   6   5   4   3

TABLE OF CONTENTS

Chapter

By the Grace of God

The Apostle Paul said, "By the grace of God, I am what I am" (I Cor. 15:10). That would seem to be an obvious truism, unnecessary even to say. But is it really? We, being ruled by our deceitful hearts, want to take credit for whatever we are, or think we are.

This collection of testimonies was prepared for two reasons: to give God the glory due unto His name and to encourage believers through a fresh realization of the mighty works of our omnipotent Christ.

God's miracle of the new birth and His supernatural provision for our earthly lives as well as our eternal souls are daily observable and continually manifest. His "wonderful works to the children of men" are in abundant supply for all to see—except those who are too busy, or too careless, to notice.

These stories of God's great grace to graduates and friends of Bob Jones University are just a few of thousands of similar stories that could be told. About sixty-eight thousand students have attended BJU during these almost seventy years. Most of them could share a compelling testimony of God's provision in saving their souls and in meeting their daily needs while they were students here.

If your soul is alive, you cannot help being thrilled and possibly even brought to tears of joy by these reminders of God's greatness and goodness manifested in these lives.

The ones whose stories you read here are people like you. What God did for them, He can do for you through His abundant grace which He sheds abroad in our hearts. Grace, of course, is favor extended which we do not deserve. It is God doing for us what we cannot do for ourselves.

In His good grace, God has allowed me the privilege for these twenty-five years to know the individuals who were kind enough to share these nuggets of God's grace so that I could pass them on to you in their own words. When you have finished reading their testimonies, perhaps you will feel that you know them too. More importantly, they hope, as I do, that you know and love the Lord, as the beneficiary of His saving and preserving grace.

Turn these pages to taste and see that the Lord is gracious.

Bob Jones III
President
Bob Jones University
1996

Special thanks to
Dave Board, Millie Butts,
Theresa Dodson, Greg Kuzmic,
Mark Sidwell, and Steve Skaggs,
valued members of the BJU "team,"
for their editing and design work.

1

A Mother's Forgotten Prayer

A Mother's Forgotten Prayer

FRANCES RINKS (ATTENDED 1951-55)

When I was a senior in high school, the Lord brought a young couple to our church and set in motion a series of events that would change the course of my life and make clear how God works out every detail of our lives in a very special way. In 1950 my small Baptist church hired a man to be youth director. Norman Riddle and his wife Vonzeal (Wall) were recent graduates of Bob Jones University and had come to Los Angeles to attend seminary and to prepare for the mission field. They later faithfully ministered many years in the Central African Republic. They were a tremendous blessing to our small group of young people, and they encouraged me to attend Bob Jones University, a Christian college I had never heard about.

For as long as I could remember, I had always wanted to go to college. In school I was an excellent student and was near the top of my class academically. In the late '40s and early '50s, high school counselors spent most of their time dealing with discipline problems; there was very little career education or college planning advice. Consequently, I had very little information about specific colleges. I knew about basic entrance requirements, but the only university I was even nominally acquainted with was the University of Oklahoma, from which my uncle had graduated. I had decided I probably would attend there.

In December 1942 my parents had come to California from Oklahoma, leaving both sets of grandparents, aunts, uncles, cousins, and so on. The oldest of three children, I loved to read (especially fairy tales) and longed to achieve success and "live happily ever after" when I grew up. My family was poor; my father was an alcoholic. Constant discord, violence, and embarrassment were the norm in our household. My mother was a wonderful Christian whose love and sacrifice gave my two sisters and me the only

3

security we had. From the age of fourteen, I worked part-time to help with my family's finances. There were seemingly no resources for college expenses, and my mother depended on me emotionally as I grew older and as my father's drinking problem became worse. I had never come to grips with the actual details of leaving home or paying tuition. I just knew I had to go to college.

Norman and Von had a wonderful ministry with the youth in our church. As they shared their experiences at BJU, I began to feel like their school was the answer to all my dreams. It was a Christian institution, offered music for no extra charge (I loved to sing in the choir), had low tuition, and allowed students to work on campus to help pay expenses. It seemed perfect, but I could imagine my mother's reaction when I told her I wanted to go to a college that was nearly twenty-three hundred miles away!

I'll never forget her response when I blurted out the news that I wanted to go to Bob Jones University in Greenville, South Carolina. With a strange expression on her face, she asked me if the school had once been called Bob Jones College and had been located in Tennessee. I told her I thought it had been, and she told me to sit down while she told me a story.

When I was a baby in Oklahoma, she had listened to Dr. Bob Sr.'s radio program from the Tennessee campus. He talked about his school: how his "boys and girls" there were protected, received a quality education with music and culture, and were taught the Bible and how to live the Christian life. As she carried me around on her hip while doing her housework and listening to the broadcast, she prayed that someday I would be able to go there to college. Every day she listened and dreamed dreams for her little daughter's future.

During World War II my father decided to move to California. As the years passed and my father's drinking continued, my mother gradually forgot about the school in Tennessee. Most of her hopes and dreams were unfulfilled, and daily living was a struggle.

Unexpectedly, I had come home and announced that I wanted to go to the very college that she had prayed I would attend. She was thrilled at the way God had brought the impossible to pass. She had forgotten, but He had not! She assured me that she would do everything she could to make it possible for me to go. Since so many of her early plans for her family had ended in disappointment, she was determined that this opportunity would succeed.

Employed as a full-time cafeteria worker in the public school system, my mother added a job as a clerk in the yardage department at Newberry's Variety Store to bring in added income, working Monday, Thursday, and Friday nights plus Saturday and Sunday. I won a $300 scholarship at school which paid for my first month's room and board, tuition, books, and train fare. (Times have changed!) Because of the work-loan scholarship program, I was able to work in the Records Office to help with the finances. Using the monthly payment plan, my mother was able to scrape together enough money from her extra job to meet the bills. God always provided.

The fall day in 1951 that I was to leave for BJU, my father got drunk. Just before time to drive to the train station, Daddy decided he needed one more drink. Unable to find any liquor in the house, he left in the car to go to the local bar. In spite of our pleas, he drove off, promising to be right back. My packed trunk, suitcases, overnight case, and food basket (fried chicken, chocolate chip cookies, and more) were already in the car. Unfortunately, he didn't return, and we were forced to call a friend to take me to Union Station. All I had were my purse and ticket; everything else was in the car. My mother waited for my father, hoping he would return in time to bring my luggage before the train left. Sadly, he was too late! My mother was unable to say goodbye to the daughter who would be gone until school was out the following May. She cried for a week!

However, I was too excited to be upset, although I soon realized how little money I had to replace the missing items: food, toothbrush, toothpaste, change of clothing, and so on. I wore the same clothes (on the train, to classes, to meals—everywhere) for nearly ten days because my trunk and suitcases did not arrive until I had been on campus a week. Roommates loaned such things as towels, bedding, pillows, and other necessary items, but none of the girls was five-foot-nine-inches tall or wore size 9½N shoes. I will never forget how thrilled I was to hear the loud announcement, "Man in the hall," as Lee Dochterman delivered my trunk to my dorm. I never wore that brown taffeta dress again!

Nothing could have spoiled those first weeks on campus. I loved everything about BJU—the beautiful campus, the friendly students, church and Vespers, the family-style meals in the Dining Common, the classes, my job in the Records Office, the caring teachers, even my crowded dorm room with my perch on the top of a triple bunk bed. The atmosphere of peace and serenity was a welcome change from the conflict and turmoil at home.

I also met my husband at BJU. During my freshman year, I was assigned to a table in the dining room where six of the eight students were from California. My mother had been concerned that I would fall in love and marry someone from Florida, the East Coast, or some other faraway state, so I looked over those California prospects with special interest. I already had several specific requirements in mind for my future husband. Besides being from California, he had to be a Christian and not drink, smoke, gamble, or cuss. Furthermore, he had to be tall and athletic because I was tall and loved sports. There were other criteria, but it was obvious that Lloyd Rinks met the first basic eight! However, getting him to ask me for a date was another matter. It took the year's absence from college because of being needed at home to help my ill sister to make an impression on him.

In January 1954 as I prepared to return to finish my sophomore year, I became aware of a medical problem that needed attention. By now I was used to obstacles that threatened to thwart my desire to attend BJU, but a year at home in a full-time job had not dampened my enthusiasm. A week before I was to depart, I had surgery. The stitches were removed on a Friday, and I left the following day. Needless to say, the twenty-three-hundred-mile bus trip was not conducive to healing or comfort.

The first person I met that first day back on campus was Lloyd. He said he hadn't seen me around for a while; I told him I had been gone for a year. He wrote a note asking me for a date to the Valentine's Banquet, then a basketball game, church, and Vespers. Soon we were engaged. God had used that year's absence from school as the catalyst for romance!

As a final confirmation of God's perfect planning and direction for my life, I was selected to sing in the radio quartet for Dr. Bob Sr.'s daily broadcast. Five mornings a week I sang with Charlotte Henwood, soprano; Dorris Norman, tenor; and Bruce Washburn, bass—just like those long-ago students had sung and inspired my mother. It was thrilling to sing the program's theme song, "All for Jesus," as well as another hymn, and to listen to Dr. Bob's message, wondering if other hopeful mothers and future students were tuned in and being challenged. The semester quickly passed, and soon I was going home again.

At the end of the summer I realized that I did not have the money needed to travel back to South Carolina or to pay for my first month's board, room, and tuition, plus books. My summer job checks had been used to help pay the family bills. I still felt strongly that God wanted me to return to BJU, so I prayed for a miracle. One day as I tried to think of someone who could supply the money, my high school civics teacher's name popped into my head. He had always encouraged me to go to college, but I had had no contact with him since I graduated three years earlier in a senior class of 540. I knew only that he had lived in Pasadena, so I dialed information. He had an unusual first and last name, so I knew I had the right person when the operator gave me a phone number.

Prayerfully, I called and asked him if he would lend me three hundred dollars so I could return to college. I explained the circumstances and told him that I would pay him back when I graduated. He agreed, and several days later I drove to Pasadena, signed a loan agreement, and received the money. Once more I happily got on the bus for the long trip with the knowledge that God would see me through.

I was unable to go back to BJU after my junior year (1954-55) because of continuing family problems. Lloyd also left in 1955 with only one semester lacking to complete his degree; he had enrolled the second semester of 1952. We were married after I graduated in 1956 from California State University—Los Angeles, and that fall I began my teaching career. Lloyd worked at Green Oak Ranch Boys' Camp and subsequently served as a youth director. However, he went back to BJU alone in January 1959 as an "old" married man of twenty-six, lived in the dorm, and graduated in May 1959 while I stayed in California and continued teaching. Returning home, he once again began serving the Lord in the ministry. The Lord later blessed us with two wonderful sons, two special daughters-in-law, and six precious grandchildren. Both families love and honor the Lord and give us much joy.

I cannot put into words how grateful I am for Bob Jones University. Because of the University, I received an excellent education that prepared me to be a high school English teacher. The lessons I learned from chapel and Bible classes taught me how to live the Christian life. The practical emphasis made me a better wife, mother, and grandmother. God has blessed me much more than I deserve or ever dreamed possible. All things have worked out for good in ways that I never imagined. God has given me the desires of my heart and used Bob Jones University as the primary agent in determining God's will for my life.

2

Little Emissaries of Satan

Little Emissaries of Satan
K. Q.

My mother was saved in her early teens. In her mid-twenties she met and married my father who, though a moral man, was not a Christian. She did this knowing full well that the marriage was not in the Lord's will. Two years later I was born, and from that day forward I was taken to church and Sunday school by my mother, but my father never attended.

When I was ten years old, I had an appendicitis attack, and I was rushed into surgery to have the appendix removed. The doctor was smiling as he came into the waiting room to give a report to my parents. When they asked why he was smiling, he replied that when I went under the anesthetic, I swore more fluently in two languages than the doctor had ever heard from a grown man. While this caused my father to smile also, it revealed to my mother that the church attendance was not having the effect that she had hoped. At that point, she began to pray earnestly that something would happen to bring me to Christ.

Some time later, my mother was in a waiting room and picked up a magazine. On the back cover was an advertisement for a school called Bob Jones University. She had never heard of the school before, but her eyes were drawn to a statement at the bottom of the ad which said, "Stands without apology for the old-time religion and the absolute authority of the Bible." She said to herself immediately, "That is where the Lord wants me to send my son to college," and she began to direct her prayers to that end without telling me or anyone else.

During my junior year in high school, the house which we were renting changed hands, and the new owners decided that they would like to live in it. They gave us notice that we would have to move by the end of June. My mother used this opportunity to tell my father that she had found a college that was inexpensive where I could attend for two years before I went to pre-med school. Since my early elementary school days, my heart's desire—and my father's for me—was to study medicine. My father saw the good sense in this proposal, since we had no funds. I had always understood that I would have to work my way through school, and Bob Jones University had a work program which fit the scenario nicely. Then my mother began to press upon my father that it would be a good idea for me to go to Bob Jones Academy as a preparatory year to the University. I was going to have to change high schools anyway because we were planning to move to a nearby state that summer. Surprisingly, my father agreed to this without hesitation.

At school the next day, I told my girlfriend (who was a member of our church) that I was going to Bob Jones Academy in the fall. Instantly, she began to tell me all the things that I would not be able to do if I attended Bob Jones. A friend of hers was attending the Academy and had nothing good to say about the place. The girl went home and told her mother who, in turn, told her brother (my Sunday school teacher). This man evidently told everyone in the church about our decision, since for the next few weeks—until we moved away—there was a steady procession of deacons, elders, the preacher, the teacher, the Sunday school superintendent, and other assorted church officials who begged my mother to send me to one of "our" schools—the denomination to which we belonged. The more people knocked on the door with stories of doom and gloom about my future if I attended this "Fundamentalist hothouse," the more determined my mother became that the Lord wanted me there. Of course, since I wanted nothing to do with any "religion" that would interfere with my current lifestyle, I rebelled and did everything I could think of to thwart these plans. Mother stood firm.

On the appointed day, I was put on the train for the overnight ride to Greenville, South Carolina. Just a few minutes after the train began to move, the girlfriend of my girlfriend searched me out and filled my ears with what I was about to encounter. This little emissary of Satan fixed my determination to get out of the predicament as early as possible.

Late in the evening, a large group of students came through the train, heading for the observation car at the rear of the train. They collected all the students that were going to Bob Jones University for a time of "fellowship." Not knowing what this meant, I joined in for what I hoped were some festivities by some unchaperoned students. To my utter dismay, when we arrived at the observation car, these students, unhindered by adult supervision, began to sing hymns. I had never seen anything like this in my life, and they were absolutely joyous about the whole affair. Then someone suggested having testimonies—whatever that was—and, unbidden, the students (about fifty of them) began going around the circle, each one of them—*every* one of them—telling of the Lord and His working in his life. For the next half hour, I kept moving stealthily around in the rear of that circle so I would not be called upon. Although I seemed to be successful at this, I now suspect that all knew what was happening, though no one challenged me.

The next evening, after supper in the Dining Common, Dr. Jones Sr. preached a sermon that placed me between heaven and hell and left me with a choice. I did not go forward at the invitation, but by my bed that night, alone with my mother's Bible, I chose heaven as my eternal home by the grace of God and the blood of the Lord Jesus Christ. From that point on, there were many growing pains, but the Christian example and discipline of a godly staff and faculty and a "hot chapel platform" molded my life, and the young man who had once said, "They are going to try to make a preacher of me in that awful place," is an ordained preacher and a staff member of Bob Jones University and rejoicing in the opportunity to mold other lives in turn.

3

Clay in the Potter's Hands

Clay in the Potter's Hands

RUSSELL P. REACH (ATTENDED 1979-82)

Jeremiah 18:1-6: "The word which came to Jeremiah from the Lord, saying, Arise, and go down to the potter's house, and there I will cause thee to hear my words. Then I went down to the potter's house, and, behold, he wrought a work on the wheels. And the vessel that he made of clay was marred in the hand of the potter: so he made it again another vessel, as seemed good to the potter to make it. Then the word of the Lord came to me, saying, O house of Israel, cannot I do with you as this potter? saith the Lord. Behold, as the clay is in the potter's hand, so are ye in mine hand, O house of Israel."

If you fill in my name there, then you have the story of my life—and really the story of any Christian's life. Here we are, a bunch of lumps of clay, and we are spinning around on this wheel. God is working, working, working, trying to make a vessel that is useful to Him, but it may not be what we want to be. We kind of squirm around because we want to be a different kind of vessel, and in trying to be something else we become marred in the hands of the potter. So what does he do here in verse four? He takes the clay and squashes it down, and he starts over. Notice that he does not throw away the clay but takes the same raw material he had and reworks it and makes it into a vessel that seems good to him. That is what happened to me.

When I was nineteen, I had become invincible. I was a sophomore pre-med major at a state university in Ohio. I had been Freshman of the Year the year before. I maintained a 4.0 GPA. I was president of my dorm, recipient of various merit scholarships and honors, and on my way, I thought, to a lucrative medical career. God looked down at me and said, "Hey, buddy, you are a lump of clay, and you have some serious flaws"; so He flattened me and started again.

What had happened was that I was dealing drugs from my dorm room. We had a big can of pot in the room, and we were selling a lot and smoking a lot. By the middle of the year, the drugs caught up with me. I went from being a four-point student to a dropout in one semester. I ended up in the hospital. I was there only a couple of weeks, but it took me months to get to the point where I could even function. God put me in a place where the only way out was up.

That summer, Beth (my wife who was my girlfriend at the time) and I traveled the country with Doug Henning and his World of Magic. When we came back from that trip, my brother (who had been an addict) and all of my friends from Miami University in Ohio were meeting in my parents' basement. They were having a youth group meeting. They had all been saved while we were gone. They were carrying Bibles and wearing regular clothes and had short hair, and my girlfriend and I walked in on this unlikely scene.

Some years earlier, during high school, I had been to a youth rally around the steps of the state capitol building in Columbus. There I had heard the salvation testimony of a young man named Franky, a victim of cerebral palsy who was wheelchair-bound and barely understandable. I had been deeply moved by his testimony at that time, but I had resisted. Now Franky was in my parents' basement speaking to this group. The power of his testimony was overwhelming. I responded to that. My mother had taught me things over the years, but I had wanted to be my own vessel, and I had drifted away and ignored those things. But the things she taught me came back, and I said, "Yes, this is true. This is where cosmic relevance is," and that was what I wanted. I was a child of the '60s, "Flower Power," Vietnam protester. (I can still use the word "groovy" correctly in a sentence.) In those years I learned how to argue a position and take a position. Every position I took was wrong, but I took a position with passion, and God used that later in my ministry.

So God squashed me and began to rebuild me. I got saved that summer. My girlfriend was saved the same week. We were baptized at the same service. Mrs. Davis, the lady who led me to the Lord, said, "OK, it is time to get married." We got married six weeks after that in September 1978. The lady came back to me and said, "It is time to go to Bob Jones University. You need to get out of this place." I said, "OK." At this point in my life, I was just taking orders because by then I didn't know what I was doing. I was just happy to be alive. I was a foot soldier taking orders.

So I got into my old beat-up, hippie Renault. My wife had wrecked it on our wedding day, so I had cranked out the front with a car jack and had bolted a 2" x 10" wooden bumper on the front. I nailed the license plate on and drove down to Greenville. I showed up on campus with a big blond Afro. I had ripped blue jeans and a flowery shirt. I parked my junky Renault and walked around the campus, but there was nobody there—not one person. You see, the problem was that it was chapel time, and everyone on campus was in the Amphitorium. So I am walking around with my big Afro and saying, "What was that they told me about the rapture? I have missed it!" But I was standing right outside the Amphitorium at 11:45 when six thousand people came out of the building. I am standing there with my big Afro, my flowery shirt, and my blue jeans, and all of these people are rushing by me, all going the same direction. They all have short hair and ties or dresses on and are all going to lunch. Nobody even saw me. I was invisible. I said, "OK," and got back into my little hippie Renault and drove back to Ohio. My new wife said, "What did you think?" I said, "Been there. Not going to do it. Wouldn't be prudent!" We filled out the BJU application in a sardonic fashion and threw it away.

But God and Mrs. Davis said, "You are going there, or you are going to die." By this time the Renault was dead, and we had an old Javelin. We took all the seats out of the Javelin and the Renault. We hooked up the wooden bumper on the Renault to the back of the Javelin, took our kitchen table and put it on the roof of the Javelin, and we stacked the seats from the car on the kitchen table and tied them up there. We stuffed all of our worldly belongings into the two cars and climbed in with just enough room to sit down. We took off and got to Cincinnati to spend Christmas at the home of my new in-laws, and you have to know they loved me by this point. "First he is a drug addict, and now he is a religious nut, and he is taking our little girl to Jim Jones University!"

We had to get to BJU for second-semester registration. We didn't have a lot of support from either family. I needed taillights on the back car because, you see, there were no taillights. There was nothing open because it was late Christmas, and I had no wire to do this with; but my father-in-law had a set of Christmas lights. So I draped the Christmas lights from the front car to the back car and wired up the car and had Christmas lights as taillights! We got into the car ready to go to Bob Jones. We went ten feet and got a flat tire, so I got out and changed the tire. It was snowing like crazy. Beth was out there getting sick in the snow because, although we didn't know it, she was already expecting our first child. I changed the tire, my wife was sick to her stomach, my mother-in-law was standing in the door crying, and we had a sign on the back, "Car in tow." We had ninety dollars, and we were off!

I had to stop several times for Beth to get sick. We made it to Asheville, and the muffler fell off the Javelin. I said, "Honey, I think we can make it. I think I can fix this." I took a cable I had in the trunk and wrapped it around the car and tied it at the top with a shoestring. I put my foot against the car and pulled the cable up, and that lifted the muffler up. I stuffed several paperback books in there and crawled in the window, and we came on down.

We pulled up at the Wade Hampton Motel, and the guy behind the desk was a BJU student—Dan McCandless. I learned later that he was leading music at Faith Baptist Church. I walked in with my big hair and flowery shirt. He looked out there and saw the car, and then he looked at me. I said, "Hi! I'm here to go to Bob Jones University." He said, "Great!" He got us a room, called us up a little later and had us over to his house the next day. Dan took me to fix the muffler. Ten bucks gone, twenty bucks for the motel; we are now down to sixty bucks. He took me to get a haircut—five dollars more! I walked into the Wade Hampton barber and said, "Hi! I'm here to go to Bob Jones University." The man just smiled at me, got the big shears out, and started cutting. He said, "Do you want to keep your sideburns?" I said, "Yes." He said, "Hold out your hand!"

That is how God got us to Bob Jones. The first day we were there, my wife found us a place to live. We had fifty-five dollars left. The very first day we had a place to live, free of charge—no rent, no room, no board—with a man who needed somebody to stay with him. God took care of us. We were able to call our parents and tell them we had made it and had free room and board. We were set up. God has taken care of us in that way ever since.

This wasn't the end of the problems. I remember Dr. Wood said one time, "Here you are at a Christian university, and you are suffering tremendous spiritual adversity." I had to ask myself, "Why?" Of course, I knew why—God was still working on that vessel that was still full of flaws.

I initially signed up for the Bible program, but soon realized I was not called to a pulpit ministry. At that time the BJU/IRS case was in the national news, and I began to feel led to serve God as an attorney. My political conversion was not as rapid or dramatic as my spiritual conversion, but I gradually began to develop a biblical view of social and political issues, and by the time I graduated I had become a certified conservative. It became my goal to take the principles I was learning and use them to have an influence at a major law school and later to become a defender of the faith through constitutional litigation.

My dream was to go back to the Boston area to study at Harvard Law School. This was a tall order, because only one other BJU graduate had ever gone to Harvard Law at that time, and my GPA had suffered from my disastrous sophomore year in Ohio. I knew the two things I could use to overcome that disability would be a good LSAT score and my interesting scope of experiences. I asked for God's help and began taking practice LSAT exams until I was scoring eight hundred (the highest score) each time. When the real thing came God went with me, and I did get the eight-hundred score. On the application, instead of downplaying my conversion from hippie-to-Christian/BJU graduate, I used it as a reason that the law school should accept me, because it made me a more diverse and unusual candidate.

Thus in 1982 I packed up Beth and our two children and headed back to Boston. Ten years after moving away from Massachusetts in the midst of the turmoil of Kent State, Watergate, and Vietnam, I was now returning as a soldier in a different war. The BJU tax case had been used as the moot court case at Harvard the year before, and some of the law school's professors had argued against BJU in the real case. The hostility toward me was often oppressive, but the principles learned at BJU and Faith Baptist Church carried us through.

Besides, I wanted to be in the battle. I wanted to be at the front lines because that is where life is exciting. That is where life is sweet. That is where life is relevant. I had done the other things. I had done the drug culture and philosopy, and I came full circle and went back to Harvard and saw it was just as vacuous as it was when I had left it.

A few years ago Beth and I and our six children moved back to Greenville, where I practice corporate law and continue my business pursuits. I have a friend from Boston here, Dave Shumate, who graduated summa cum laude from Vanderbilt and magna cum laude from Harvard Law School. He is now associate pastor at Faith Baptist Church in Greenville. He and I spent many hours up there in Boston hashing out all these things. We can defend the Bible. Our legal opinion is that the Bible is true. We have concluded that you do not have to be a nitwit to be a Christian. In fact, you have to be a nitwit not to be a Christian. If you are honest and your brain is functioning properly, you will find that this is where the truth is. This is where relevance is. The whole lifestyle we left behind is meaningless.

Dave and I continue our late night talks, and we are trying to find the time to put into a book some of the things God has taught us over these years. We are also working with others on a project to hold advanced pastoral studies seminars in Caribbean countries to assist and encourage indigenous pastors.

I am thankful God brought me directly to Bob Jones University and Faith Baptist as a young Christian so that I could learn how to turn my experiences to good for God's service and glory. Some of those experiences were very destructive and have left me permanently scarred. Some of them still limit my ministry, and I don't recommend that anyone follow the same path. On the other hand, God has used these things in my life, and I would not change anything that happened to me, "for of him, and through him, and to him, are all things" (Rom. 11:36). You have to be pliable in the hands of the Potter. You have to be willing for the Potter to make you the way He chooses.

4

A Lot to Learn

A Lot to Learn
K. L.

My parents were divorced when I was five years old. My mother immediately moved our family to Florida to start a new life. My father has been out of the picture ever since. After moving to Florida, my mom soon remarried, and that marriage lasted only six years.

It was soon after the second divorce that our home life really began to deteriorate. At this time, I was twelve years old, and over the next five years I saw a great deal of immorality taking place in my home and all around me. Without God's providential care in my life, I probably would have been a participant rather than an on-looker. Even though I had never attended church or even seen a Bible, God had His hand on my life. He chose to spare me from a lot of sin that my family participated in. I never even swore or used the Lord's name in vain. I knew there was more to this life than just the here and now. I knew there was a God out there somewhere and that somehow we were accountable for our actions.

When I was seventeen years old, I was a junior in high school. My mom could see that I was different because I didn't participate in the immoral lifestyles that surrounded me. I realized, however, that I was no angel. She decided to buy a bus ticket for me to move back up North to live with relatives we had left twelve years ago. When I arrived at the bus station, I had quite a chip on my shoulder and an attitude to go with it. But God's hand was already at work.

My relatives who picked me up that day were Christians. (Co-incidence? I don't think so. Psalm 27:10: "When my father and my mother forsake me, then the Lord will take me up.") They had only one requirement for me to be a part of their family, and that was to go to church. Church? I almost died! I knew that I had to wear a dress, and I felt I was definitely entering a foreign culture. I knew nothing about church, and I wanted no part of it; I did, however, want to finish high school and needed a place to live, so I went.

After attending church with them for about nine months, Evangelist Jerry Sivnksty came for a week of special meetings. During that week in April, I was not paying attention (as usual), but it was as if God reached down and poked me and said, "Pay attention; this is for you." On April 19, 1977, Jerry Sivnksty made this statement: "The most righteous person you know will still bust hell wide open when he dies if he does not know Jesus Christ as his personal Savior." He was describing me. I heard nothing else. That was enough for me to meet him after church and ask him how I could be saved. Mr. Sivnksty graciously led me to Christ that night.

When I got home, my relatives wanted to talk to me about the decision I had made at church and the impact it would have on my life. During the conversation, it came up that I was eighteen years old and now legally an adult. I really had a lot to learn about the Christian life in a short amount of time. Therefore, they recommended that I go to a Christian college. College? That wasn't quite in my plans! But I listened. They listed a few colleges they approved of, and one of them was Bob Jones University.

After graduating from high school, we soon began to visit colleges. BJU was the first and the last college we visited. I knew that was where God wanted me to be. I went to the Administration Building to fill out an application, and Mr. David Christ, Director of Admissions, met me in the hallway and asked if he could help me. I told him, "I would like to go here." He said, "We would love to have you come." The reason I am very touched by this incident is that I was not dressed like I was going to church. I had on old blue jeans and a T-shirt, and nothing about me looked very desirable. I had nothing to offer, but he never batted an eye or made me feel like, "Boy, do you have a lot to learn!" BJU is special to me because they allow Christ to make a difference, and they give everyone that chance.

Three months later I was at Bob Jones University. What a culture shock! I thought wearing a dress twice a week to church was bad. Now they told me I had to wear one every day! I really thought they were joking—but they weren't. Then to wear a hat on Sundays—that almost put me over the edge. Remember, I had been saved only about four months before coming to BJU.

My first Bible class was New Testament Survey. The first day of class the teacher said, "Turn to the book of Matthew." I thought to myself, "Wait, that wasn't on the book list, and I didn't buy that book!" So I just sat there. Finally, the guy sitting next to me leaned over and said, "You do know that's in your Bible, don't you?" I thought, "Why didn't he say so!" Experiences like these at the beginning of school really made me wonder what I was doing at BJ. I felt out of my league. But God's Word says, "My grace is sufficient for thee: for my strength is made perfect in weakness" (II Cor. 12:9). The Lord graciously sustained me because of the prayers and support of many of His people. As a result of this, I was able to graduate from BJU with a B.S. in elementary education.

God is so good! I'm so glad. "But God hath chosen the foolish things of the world to confound the wise; and God hath chosen the weak things of the world to confound the things which are mighty; and base things of the world, and things which are despised, hath God chosen, yea, and things which are not, to bring to nought things that are: that no flesh should glory in his presence. But of him are ye in Christ Jesus, who of God is made unto us wisdom, and righteousness, and sanctification, and redemption: that, according as it is written, He that glorieth, let him glory in the Lord" (I Cor. 1:27-31).

The Lord has blessed me in many, many ways since I became His child. I've been married for almost fourteen wonderful years, and I have a six-year-old boy, a three-year-old boy with Down syndrome, and one on the way! "What?" you say. "Down syndrome? How can you say God has blessed you?" Actually, this little guy has been one of the greatest blessings God has ever allowed me to experience. To be honest, we all could learn a few lessons from his simple ways and childlike faith. God makes no mistakes! Luke 12:48b says, "For unto whomsoever much is given, of him shall be much required." I certainly am one to whom much has been given.

5

Do It Now

Do It Now

W. C. HATHCOCK, M.D.

In the fall of 1966, as an eye, ear, nose, and throat specialist, I routinely drove to St. Joseph Hospital in Atlanta every morning. On my drive about eight o'clock each morning, I listened to Dr. Bob Sr., who had a program on radio station WAVO. One day he stated, "You can know all of the Bible and about the Lord Jesus Christ and still go to hell," and this really got my attention. He said, "You must recognize you are a sinner and that Jesus paid that sin debt, but most importantly, you must make it personal. You must invite Christ into your heart and let Him be Lord of your life. And if you have never done this, do it now."

I pulled the car over to the curb and asked the Lord to come into my heart and save me.

When I arrived home that afternoon, my wife greeted me saying, "I was saved this morning when I listened to Dr. Bob Sr." Then I told her of my experience, and what a time of rejoicing we had that afternoon!

Since that day, our lives have been completely changed. The worldly things have lost their glitter, our associates have changed, and our lifestyles are completely different. We are rejoicing in our Savior, believing Him to be faithful as He said He would in His Word.

"But the Lord is faithful, who shall stablish you, and keep you from evil" (II Thess. 3:3).

We often thank the Lord for Bob Jones University and its staff and what it has meant to us. Your stand for righteousness, holiness, and godly living has been a standard that we believe is pleasing to God our Savior.

6

God Will Lead, and I Will Follow

God Will Lead, and I Will Follow

ZLATKA "DIMI" DIMITROVA (ATTENDED 1992-)

"Delight thyself also in the Lord; and he shall give thee the desires of thine heart." (Psalm 37:4)

It was Easter time again—our favorite time of the year. Next to Christmas, this was the most important holiday for me. This year I was graduating from high school, and I wondered if Grandpa Jordan would say something about that. My grandpa was a special kind of person. He never talked too much, but when he talked, everyone listened. He strongly disliked lazy kids, and we grandkids tried to do our best when helping him for fear that he would become upset and give us a long sermon. Two of his sermons, though, we enjoyed a lot, and I remember them vividly because we heard them every year, over and over again. I still do not become tired of hearing those. One sermon he told us at Christmas. It was about the birth and life of our Lord Jesus Christ. The second one was about His last days on earth, His crucifixion and resurrection. This one was my most favorite story, and this one we were going to hear at lunch time when the whole family gathered around the table.

Grandma Elena was moving quite fast getting the meal ready for everybody. She was in her early sixties now, but one could hardly tell—so much energy filled her little body with life and enthusiasm for her work. Our grandparents lived quietly at the end of their small village in Bulgaria. We, their five grandchildren, often came to help them with their never-ending work. We did not mind getting up early on Easter morning. It was not just the food that excited us but also the thought of how much we owe to this wonderful holiday.

The churches were open at that time, but there was no preaching inside. The Communist government did that after World War II, and

35

even though we did not have a Communist government anymore, the churches were still considered museums. We had no problem visiting the church, but no message was preached there. We had to wait until we got home for lunch to hear that wonderful story of the resurrection and the gift of eternal life given to those who believe in Christ. Of course, I had believed it ever since I first understood it! There was nothing more beautiful and worthy of believing than the story of our Lord who humbled Himself and suffered and died for me so that I might live forever. I had repented, and I believed that with my whole heart!

That day passed just like any other Easter Sunday we had before. All these years, Grandpa had kept and quietly preserved his faith and made sure all of his children and grandchildren knew about the greatest and brightest event that ever happened in the world. We were so fortunate to have a grandfather like Grandpa Jordan.

He gave thanks to God for the food and told us the story again. We listened carefully and asked many questions, as usual. He always answered with a calm and confident voice, while staring at something on the table. Then all at once he turned toward me and asked, "Zlate, you are finishing school this year. What do you intend to do?"

"Well, you know, Grandpa, I would love to fly and be a pilot. Also, remember how I have told you that I'd like to go to America and study there?"

"All that is very good, but you know it won't be as easy to do it as it is to say it."

"I have thought of trying for the Military Aviation Academy. What do you think?"

"Never hurts to try! Indeed, it never hurts to try."

"Oh, she is not going to become a pilot. They don't accept girls to be pilots," interrupted my brother with a frown on his face. It was hard to interpret whether he was sorry for me or if he was mocking my dreams. I was well known to be a dreamer, not only in our family but also at school and among all our friends and relatives.

While I was looking at my brother and struggling to come up with a smart answer to his pessimistic remark, Grandma decided to join him. "What is it?" she exclaimed. "What is pulling you toward the skies? It is not for a girl to undertake such a profession, Zlate. It would be better if you don't torture yourself with too much thinking about such unrealistic desires. They will not let you fly in this country, can't you see?"

"Well, don't talk to her like that, Elena." My grandpa had taken up for me. "They might not let her fly in this country, but it won't hurt her to try."

"Why do you say that?" my grandma rushed to ask. "She will be so hurt and heartbroken after they turn her down! It is better that she hears it from us first. At least she will be warned what to expect."

"Oh, she is old," I thought, "and like all old people, reluctant and conservative." I could not blame her for telling me the truth, though. She was right. I knew it. Yet something inside me was telling me, "You can't stop! You have to try! It isn't over until it's over!" Besides, what would all my friends think? No, it would not be easy. I wanted to fly, and I knew that was my calling! Only Grandpa understood me fully. Still, Grandma had a valuable point. It was a daring dream—almost impossible! But I always thought anything that seemed impossible to me and everyone else was possible for the Lord, and I believed that this impossible thing would happen. It would take a miracle, it is true, but it would happen! God would help me!

"Oh, my dearest Lord, how I wish You would help me in this new calling! If I ever learn to fly, I will use it to work and start a school with money You would allow me to earn! There I would teach my students how to dream and at whose feet to lay their dreams that they may see them come true someday!" This was my only prayer since that day.

The month of May came, and high school came to an end, but with that my preparations for the future started. I was preparing to apply to the National Military Aviation Academy, the only place in Bulgaria where one could learn how to fly. At that time skydiving lessons were offered in Stara Zagora, the city where we lived, so I signed up. Each applicant for the Academy had to have at least two parachute jumps. I will never forget that first jump! There is nothing like hanging in the air, all by yourself!

After that, Mr. Georgieff, the flight instructor at that flight school, gathered together those of us who wanted to apply to the Academy and told us about all of the requirements. There were a couple of guys who gave up right then. Then Mr. Georgieff told us what day we would leave for Sofia, the capital, where the medical examinations were held. He said they usually lasted about four or five days.

We—nine guys, Mr. Georgieff, and I—left on Monday, June 10. The next day was to be our first day before the Aviation Medical Committee. For some applicants, the examinations lasted only a day; for others, two days; and for some, five days. On Tuesday two of our guys had to leave because they failed the blood tests. On the next day four others who failed different examinations returned home. On the third day one of the guys failed the eye test; another failed the pressure chamber test, and we were down to two! I went from room to room with great fear because everywhere doctors met me with unfriendliness and mockery. Each doctor was trying to tell me that flying was not for me because I was a woman. They told me that with my high school diploma, I could easily be accepted in college to study to be a doctor or a professor or whatever I wished. I listened patiently and did not dare to reply. After they had finished their messages, I would simply ask if my physical condition were good enough for flying. Every single time they answered positively, but. . . . (There was always that "but.") Finally, after I had passed all the examinations, the committee held a special session to decide my situation. After a whole hour of prayer in the hallway outside the assembly room, I had to hear the most discouraging words coming out of the president's mouth. "You are a woman, and although your physical condition is good for flying, you cannot do that because we do not accept women in the Academy," he said. Then he handed me my papers, which I accepted with tears in my eyes. He walked away unmoved.

There I stood, astonished and crushed. "But, Lord, whatever happened with all my prayers?" How many times I cried that week when going from one exam to another, enduring with a smile all the humiliation and verbal abuse from these doctors! I went on with the faith that my God would not desert me, with the hope that my prayers would be answered and that a miracle would happen! Alas, all my hopes were scattered!

I remembered then a proverb that Grandpa always told us. "When the doors are closed, God will open a window." Now a new hope filled my soul: America—that wonderful land of opportunity which I had visited last summer for the First International Space Camp in Huntsville, Alabama. Surely I could apply to study in one of the colleges with which I kept correspondence! That new idea absorbed my whole mind, and I started praying about it right away as I was sitting in the train going back home.

I wrote to Embry-Riddle Aeronautical Institute in Daytona Beach, Florida, sent all my applications, and waited patiently. Except! There was one thing—a very important thing—that I had overlooked. The money! It never occurred to me how expensive education must be in a capitalistic country. The financial aid information and application forms did not even catch my attention. I did, however, send the fifty-dollar registration fee. "It costs a lot of money to register," I thought, "but think of the education I will get for these fifty dollars!" I never thought that this could be just a very small *caparo* (Bulgarian for a non-refundable reservation fee).

In the beginning of July, an invitation from Embry-Riddle came to me. I went to Sofia to apply for a visa at the American embassy. My cousin, Daniela, came with me. We arrived in the capital early in the morning, about six o'clock. We headed straight from the railway station to the embassy. I knew that they admitted only twenty people a day to see the consul, so we had to hurry.

Around ten o'clock we walked out of the embassy with a visa in my passport. I could not believe that they gave me a visa in less than five minutes without asking me any questions. We stopped by the SwissAir bureau on our way to the train station. I asked for a reservation to the cheapest destination on the southeastern coast of America, thinking it would most certainly be cheaper to take a bus from the airport to Daytona Beach. The lady informed me that most of their flights were full, so she put me on the waiting list of two flights. The flights left for Atlanta on Monday morning, July 29, and on Tuesday, July 30. "So far so good," I thought. "Now You'll have to provide the money for the flight, Lord."

After all this, I headed to see my parents. So far I was not thinking of going away from them but only of flying. But now I realized that in order to reach this dream I had to separate from my family and that separation was going to be painful.

My grandfather had to hear the story, of course, so his village was my next stopping point. "If you find someone who will pay half of the price of your ticket, Zlate, I will give you the other half. An opportunity like this is not to be forfeited," said Grandpa. "Are you serious, Grandpa? Are you sure?" I did not know whether to believe this miracle or not, so I shouted with joy. I went back to Stara Zagora where we started looking for sponsors to pay my flight ticket to Atlanta. If I had only known this was not *all* the expense that was needed for my education in America! But I did not know, so that is why I proceeded with much faith and great expectations to "finish the job." I believe the Lord kept me ignorant of certain things so that I would not get discouraged.

I made appointments with many directors and many presidents of different companies. Alas, they all had only one answer for me, "This is just a dream, little girl. You will never be a pilot. I would suggest that you forget it and don't trouble yourself with it anymore." I just smiled politely, as if to say their advice was accepted, and left with a bitter "Thank you." Although I was calm outwardly, inside I was crushed. Realizing that I could not do any more than what had already been done, I turned my voice again to God, as Grandpa had taught me since I was little. He, my Lord, was the only One who took interest in me when everyone else had left me. He, who came to save my life before I was even born, knowing what a wretch I was, came again to help me! I placed my confidence in the Lord. Every morning as he was leaving for work, Grandpa used to say, "God will lead, and I will follow." I thought of that often and repeated it every time I left home to go for an interview.

I said that to myself again the day when I went to see Mrs. Georgieff at the school. I had to stop by the office to pick up my diploma. It was Monday—a beautiful day outside. She met me with a bright smile, and her first words were, "How is our little pilot?" Mrs. Georgieff said she had talked to the principal of the school who was a very influential person and had good connections with many firms and companies. "I told him all about you," she said, "and he promised me that he would speak to some of his friends who are managers. I know him. When he promises something, he will do it, so I know he will help you, dear."

I lost my thoughts and, without even saying a word, slid down in the chair that was placed next to me. "Oh, Lord," I prayed silently, "this is not so hard after all! I will simply follow while You do the work and the thinking for me."

There was only one week remaining until my flight. On Tuesday morning the lady from SwissAir called me and said that she canceled my first reservation because there was an open seat for the second flight and that if I wanted it, I had to buy the ticket within two days. Two days! "That is precious little time for me to come up with nine hundred dollars, Lord! I wonder how this is going to happen?"

I went to church that morning and prayed for a long time. That night my school principal, Mr. Stoyanov, called. "I've had my own business for a little over a year," he said to me on the phone, "and I have saved my profits from it to buy myself a new car. Now you are short on time. I was going to see if one of my friends could sponsor you through his company, but we don't have time. You may have these ten thousand leva that I have saved, for whether I will drive a new car or my old piece of junk does not matter to me. I will still be the same person. Now, you need this money; take it and use it." That was a lot of money in Bulgaria—a little less than what one would make in a year if he was, let's say, a teacher. We decided that I was going to stop by his office to take care of the paperwork and get the money on Thursday.

I bought the ticket Thursday afternoon and exchanged the remaining cash for $260. Everything happened so fast that I did not have time to think of what I was actually doing, nor did I think of the dangers of going somewhere alone without knowing anybody. I was not thinking, maybe, because of my lack of knowledge about life in America. Oh, but I was not going to worry about that! Who cared about such a minor detail? I told myself, "I will think of that when I get there. As for now, God will lead, and I will follow." That was the solution to all my problems.

We arrived at the airport just in time for my flight. I did not have much time to say good-bye, so we had to make this most sorrowful and hard moment as quick as possible. Mother kissed me many times and embraced me in her arms for the longest while. When was she going to see me again? How long did she have to wait to hear from me? Who was going to take care of me over there in that world which she had never seen before? She was allowing her little daughter to go—on her own? I saw all these questions in her eyes, but she did not open her mouth to speak, for she had no voice left.

After an overnight layover in Zurich, I arrived in Atlanta at five o'clock the next day. I decided to go to church and pray. I was hoping to find the pastor there and ask him for advice on how to get to Florida. But what church was I going to ask for? From what I knew, I figured that Baptist must be the closest to my grandparents' Orthodox belief, so I thought I would try that.

I got into a taxi and asked the driver if she would take me to a Baptist church. After we had traveled for quite a while, I noticed we passed Philadelphia Baptist Church a couple of times. We went on the highway and then on some smaller roads, and after a few minutes, there was Philadelphia Baptist Church again. I looked at the meter, and it was showing over fifty dollars now. The lady asked me if I had any friends there. "Yes, yes," I said, "I will stop here!" So she stopped, took my luggage from the trunk, and, after I paid her fifty dollars for the ride which acquainted me with the roads around Atlanta, she wished me "Good luck" and left.

Brother Bill was a new pastor. He had just arrived about three weeks before. He was in his early thirties and had been an evangelist for almost eight years.

After the service was over, a lady came and asked me to sit with her during prayer time. I followed her while she was telling me that her name was Kathy Butler and that this had been her church for a long time. When we sat down, most of the ladies gathered around us and started asking me questions. They started with whether I was saved and what church I attended back home and went on to how old I was and why I was here. None of them could believe how any parents could have let their eighteen-year-old daughter leave and go somewhere all by herself.

"Do you have a reservation for a hotel to spend the night?" asked Mrs. Butler. "No," was my reply. "Do you then have a vehicle?" continued Kathy, overwhelmed with curiosity. My answer was negative again. "Then where are you going to stay tonight?" she asked me. "I don't know," I said. Then she looked at me and said, "Would you like to come home with me?" Truly, I did not know what I was going to do that night, but I also was not expecting anything, and this invitation was a shock to me. Being the kind of person who would not let an opportunity pass by, I accepted. "Thank you so much," I mumbled. "This is more than I would ever have expected."

Mrs. Butler's husband approached the group of women, and Kathy said, "John, I want you to meet Zlatka Angelova Dimitrova. She is coming home with us." Mrs. Butler had just learned my whole name, and she did not let the first chance pass by without showing everybody how well she could pronounce it. This did not impress Mr. Butler though, because he shook his head at the sound of it and said gaily, "How are you doing, Betty?" I realized that it would be very hard for these poor people to try pronouncing my name all the time, so I told them that some of my friends called me "Dimi" for short. The girls from the International Space Camp in Huntsville came up with that nickname for me a year ago. I liked it because it was part of my last name, so it was not a new name, and it was also a Bulgarian name.

The Butlers took me home that night. They told me that they had three sons and three grandsons and that, although they had always wanted one, they had never had a daughter. Mr. Butler showed me to the room where I was going to spend the night. Kathy came a couple of minutes later and told me how to make my bed and that I could use the shower in the small bathroom, and then she wished me "Good night." I was so lonely, so tired, and so desperately scared! I was in the house of people I had never met before, and I had no idea what the future held.

At that moment, I heard a knock on the door. I had to wipe my tears and wash my face. It was Kathy. "I thought," she said to me, pretending not to have noticed my red eyes, "that it would be good if you called your parents and let them know that you have arrived safely." I looked at her with astonishment. "But I cannot do that," I said, "because it's very expensive to call Bulgaria from here." She told me not to worry about it but to pick up the phone and call. I did as she told me and reached my brother who was alone at home that day. I just told him that I had arrived safely and that I was going to call them again later.

The next morning Kathy called the university in Florida, and they turned me down because I did not have any money. No money! I had two hundred dollars! Was not that enough?

Then everyone thought that I would have to go back to Bulgaria. Kathy decided to keep me for a while until we found out what was going to happen next. The pastor at Philadelphia Baptist had a definite answer. "We will wait and see what the Lord is going to do. He brought her here for a reason which we don't know, but I hope we'll find out soon."

At prayer meeting the next week a missionary from Greenville, South Carolina, came to preach. Brother Bill did not know this man, whose name was Bob Hein. When he and the pastor talked on the telephone, the pastor thought he said that his name was Bob Heim, who is a missionary to the Philippines and is supported by Philadelphia Baptist. So Brother Bill told him that he was welcome to his church any time.

I had the opportunity to meet this missionary from Hampton Park Baptist Church in Greenville. He was going to Australia with his family to serve the Lord there. Some of the people had already told him my story, so I just had to confirm that I had come here to learn how to fly airplanes. A wide smile brightened his face, and he said to me, "The university from which I graduated offers an aviation program. It is a fine Christian school, too, where you could get biblical training as well as professional training in many other areas. Would you like for me to check into that?" It was a miracle! I collected myself the best I could to give him a positive answer.

That night Brother Hein called Mr. Christ, the Director of Admissions at Bob Jones University, and also Mr. Pfaffenroth, Chairman of the Aviation Department. He set up an interview for me with both of them for Friday afternoon of the same week. Mrs.

Butler said she would take me to Greenville because she wanted to see the school herself.

My first visit to Bob Jones University was on Friday, July 9, 1991. It was my first time ever to visit a Christian college. Everything looked so lovely—the buildings, the streets, the flowers, the trees. The whole campus exhibited such brightness and beauty beyond belief. I also fell in love with the airport and the little airplanes that the students fly. When was I going to get in one of those? I liked this place! I thought I would be very privileged if the Lord should open the door for me to come and study here.

So I applied for admission that day. But we had to go back to Georgia and wait, pray, and hope that soon I would return here to be a flight student.

The time passed by fast. In the fall I was able to attend and audit some of the classes at Philadelphia Christian School. Mrs. Butler thought this would be very helpful for me to prepare me for college. I had studied English since I was four years old, but it was more difficult to hear and comprehend than it was to read and understand.

Some of the people from Smyrna Presbyterian Church in Conyers tried to send me to Berry College in Rome, Georgia. So in October, Mr. and Mrs. Butler took me there to visit the school. It was very beautiful, and I fell in love with the campus. But they did not offer aviation! It is so interesting how the Lord used my dream of flying to direct me to the right place He had prepared for me.

It was mid-December, and we were getting ready for Christmas. We still did not know where I was going to school, but I waited patiently.

One day John and I were working in the yard when Kathy rushed out of the house. She was shouting as loudly as she could at us. We stopped our work and looked at her with amazement. "Hey, Dimi, John, guess what? You will never believe this! The telephone just rang, and guess who it was? You wouldn't believe it! A man from Bob Jones University. I had already put that school out of my mind, but guess what he said?"

We found out that while we were patiently waiting in Georgia, the administration at Bob Jones University was praying for me that the Lord would provide a way for me to go to school there. How strange! I had never heard of a school before whose staff and instructors took such great interest in prospective students! Then Kathy said they had decided to give me a scholarship and that I could go to school there in January. That was in less than a month!

When we visited the school, our pastor said that it would be a "Red Sea" miracle if I went to study there. Truly, the bill was quite high because it included flight instruction, but the Lord took care of that. Everyone at church was astonished when Mrs. Butler related her conversation with Mr. Schatz from the Admissions Office at BJU.

Kathy and John helped me pack and took me to school. On Tuesday, January 14, of the year 1992, I arrived on campus—as a student this time. Please believe me, it was a very special feeling—a feeling of comfort that comes from knowing that you are in the will of God. Doubts were going to come later, but the Lord was always there to help me to overcome them and feel that blessed comfort again.

This was the day of the beginning of my studies—and not only in flying. I had to take a double major—Business and Commercial Aviation—because flying was not offered by itself. It was also the beginning of learning more about the Bible and about life. In the classrooms and in chapel we were to be taught how to live for our Lord. Then in the dormitory, we were to learn how to apply this knowledge. Above all, I had to begin working on my patience. Yes, after waiting for five months to find out what school was in my future, I still had to learn patience.

A few days after I arrived at school, on Monday, January 20, was my first flight lesson. Mr. Burke, my first flight instructor, showed me how to make a preflight check on the airplane. Then he said to me, "You will be sitting at the left side. You start flying as a pilot from your first lesson."

Lined up with the central line of the runway and cleared by the controller for takeoff, we advanced the throttle, released the brakes, and gradually lifted off the ground. With this, my dream became true. After each hour of flying, I liked it more than before. I never grew tired of it.

Since then, every time I roll down the runway and take off in an airplane, the thought of how fortunate I am and how gracious our Lord is comes to my mind. This story, then, is my constant reminder that I could not have realized any of my dreams, nor could I have learned alone any of the things I am now enjoying. It is because of His mercy, love, and faithfulness that all this happened to me. It can happen to anybody. It is a testimony of God's power to work in our lives and to help us so that we may glorify Him and learn to wait on Him.

"But they that wait upon the Lord shall renew their strength; they shall mount up with wings as eagles; they shall run, and not be weary; and they shall walk, and not faint." (Isaiah 40:31)

7

The Prison Guard's Son

The Prison Guard's Son
S. D.

I was born into a Christian home October 28, 1954. My parents were born-again Christians who desired to live for the Lord and reared their children according to the Word of God the best they knew how. I was one of eight children who received a Christian education. My parents were members of a nondenominational Bible church, and I was in a Christian school until sixth grade. It was at that time there were some changes in our family life. The family situation, no doubt, was very difficult for my parents as my father was a prison guard for over twenty years. That and other reasons caused our parents to put us in a public school. I began public school in seventh grade, and there were influences there that I never was able to resist—never wanted to resist. I wasn't a Christian, and I lived like the world.

It was in the seventh grade that I first got involved in what would be called "light" drugs. I began sniffing glue, smoking marijuana, drinking beer, and generally wanting to have fun—a lot of amusement with little or no thought of God or His Word. I had no desire to please God; I lived only to please myself. As I began to experiment with drugs, it wasn't long before I moved on to harder drugs. I began shooting drugs—meth and heroin. By the time I was seventeen years old, I was a heroin addict. I dropped out of school once I was able to and began to support my habit through burglaries and other avenues of criminal activity: stealing cars, stealing whatever I could get my hands on, and working with a gang in order to support my drug addiction. As a member of a street gang in Philadelphia, I was also involved in gang warfare. Many were the nights that we went to fight gangs from other parts of the city. I prided myself in the fact that I was a gang member, and no doubt I found great security in being part of that group—being wild, living my life without any restraint and without any authority.

I was arrested as a juvenile, but I did not go to the prison where my father worked in the city of Philadelphia; instead I went to a place reserved for juvenile delinquents. My father told me one time, "Steve, if you get locked up again, I am not coming after you. You are going to stay there." So when I was arrested again at the age of seventeen and still under the legal responsibility of my parents, I lied about my age. I was arrested for drug possession and for carrying a concealed deadly weapon. I lied about my age because I feared that my father would not come to get me. I said I was eighteen, figuring that perhaps I would have a low bail set and would be able to get out on my own—that my friends would help me to get out. The bail was set at one thousand dollars, and I needed another hundred dollars in order to be set on conditional liberty until the time of the trial. I didn't have the money, and none of my friends came through with the money, so I was sent to the prison (called a detention center) in Philadelphia where my father worked. Up until this point I hadn't told anyone my dad was a prison guard (especially the prisoners I was with), fearing retaliation.

As we pulled up to the gates of the prison and were getting out, I said to one of the drivers of the police van, "My father works here." Obviously, they would not allow me to go in. The prisoners who were with me overheard me talking to the guard and understood then that I was the son of a prison guard. The other prisoners were dropped off there; I was taken to another prison in the city in order not to be where my father worked, which was against prison policy. My dad had always been a great witness in the prison and was respected for his testimony. Often he was called "the preacher." You can imagine the sorrow and brokenheartedness that he felt when the next day when he arrived at work there were prisoners who said, "Hey, Mr. ____, your son was with us last night. We saw him. He is now over at the House of Correction." No doubt that was a very difficult experience for my father. There were prisoners who said to my dad, "How do you expect us to listen to you if your own son doesn't listen to you?"

I began selling heroin. I found it was more lucrative not only to support my habit but also to procure for myself those outward trappings I desired to have—a nice car, girlfriends, jewelry. As I began selling heroin, I was able to develop a fairly successful business in Philadelphia. I bought a Cadillac and rode around like a "big shot." I thought at that time that I was "something"—and in the eyes of my friends I was. In their eyes I had "made it." I had all the money I wanted and the so-called friends I wanted. Looking back on my human existence, it was at this time in my life that I really sank to the pit where there was nothing I would not do. There was no avenue of pleasure I would not try. I lived a very profligate life and knew that what I was doing was wrong.

Even though I was not a Christian, I could not escape what I had heard over the years—what my parents had taught me, what I had heard in church, and the songs I learned. I did not deny that God existed. I believed that Jesus died on the cross for my sins, but I had no place for Him in my life. As I look back, I can see a number of times when the hand of God in my life clearly protected me from myself and from the Evil One. More than once I overdosed on drugs and had to be revived; if someone hadn't been there at the time, I probably would have died. I would have passed out into eternity lost and would be in hell today. I can remember very clearly the time I overdosed in my own home, in my own bedroom. I woke up one morning and gave myself an injection of heroin. The next thing I remember was my father yelling at me. My mother had come into the room as I lay there overdosed and saw I was already changing colors. She ran out of the room and yelled to my father. She said, "Jim, I think Steve is dead!" At that time my dad came into the room, picked me up, took the needle out of my arm, and began slapping me in order to revive me. So there are those occasions I look back upon that bring fear into my life as I remember how close I came to leaving this world without Christ.

In 1970 my brother John was led to Jesus Christ by my father. I saw a great change in his life. It was undeniable—the testimony he had as God delivered him from drug addiction as well. John went to Bob Jones University. In many ways I was glad to be rid of him because whenever he was around me he bothered me. He bothered me because he was always memorizing verses or talking to me about the Lord. So when he went to Bob Jones, it gave me some peace so I could continue my existence without his interference.

Also while he was gone, I was able to sell some of his possessions. I sold a radio of his and other things he left behind. They were gone when he came back on Christmas vacation. But John had a real burden for me. He loved me and prayed for me. My parents prayed for me. They believed God was able to save me, although there were many others who doubted. There were friends of my parents, members of the same church, who told them that I had gone too far and that I would never come back. My parents did not believe that, so they continued to pray. John prayed, and every time he came home he prayed for me and talked to me and loved me. I did not want to listen to the gospel. There were times when I would yell at him, even strike out physically at him. I remember very clearly one time I grappled with him in order to try to shut him up, to quiet him, because I didn't want to hear what he had to say. Yet he persevered in his love for his lost brother.

In December of 1973 before coming home for Christmas vacation, John gave a testimony before the entire student body and requested prayer for me. He wanted to go home that Christmas to win his brother to Jesus Christ. It so happened that my wife (that is, the woman who is now my wife) was a student at Bob Jones and heard John's testimony and his desire to win his brother to Christ.

On December 16, 1973, my brother was in a Sunday evening church service, but he left the church before the service was over and came running home through the snow with a heart that was broken for me. He came running into the house crying as I was sitting there watching television. I was waiting for some of my drug buddies to come so we could go and make a buy. It was not the night I intended to come to Christ. That was the furthest thing from my mind. But when John came in with such a broken heart, I was moved, yet I wanted to be left alone. I will never forget what John said to me: "Steve, won't you come to Christ? I can't help but feel that something is going to happen to you." I didn't respond. I wasn't ready to respond. My brother left our living room and went upstairs to the bedroom. He went there to pray.

As I sat there, I thought about my condition, my spiritual misery, and I realized how much I needed Jesus Christ as my Savior. I got up out of my chair and walked up the stairs into the bedroom. My brother was there kneeling and crying. He looked up at me, perhaps wondering what I was doing. I broke down and said, "Oh, John, pray with me. I need to get saved." We both were on our knees that night before God as I cried and repented of my sin and opened my heart to Jesus Christ. The first thing John wanted to do was to take me back to church, so we got into my car and drove to church. The service was not yet over. There was a Christmas program that night, and there was not a regular invitation, but at the end of the service I walked up to see my parents who were at the front of the church. As I made my way down the aisle, I could feel eyes fixed on me, looking at my long hair down over my shoulders and the way I was dressed. The people were wondering, "What is Steve doing here?" I walked up to my parents. No doubt they were as surprised as anyone else, and I said, "I got saved tonight." Soon not only my parents but friends from the church were gathered around crying and praising the Lord for what God had done in my life.

God began to change my life through the Word, through prayer, through the help of friends, and through churches where I was active. It was not always easy. I was still a drug addict, but God gave me victory over drug addiction. I went to methadone clinics day after day in order to receive methadone, but God did what they could not do for me. He delivered me from drugs.

A short time later I moved to the Midwest to live with a pastor's family that later became my brother's in-laws. They invited me to live with them in order to get away from the life I was living and from the friends who, even though I was saved, would still come to my house at all hours of the night asking and sometimes begging for drugs. They were begging me to go and make a contact, but, of course, I could not do that any more. I went to the Midwest with some real reservations and fears. I had already cut my hair one time after I got saved, but Pastor said that in order to live with him I needed to get a real haircut, which I did. He laid down some rules. If I smoked (which I still did at the time), I couldn't smoke in the house, so I would go outside to catch a smoke from time to time. Yet I began to grow. I was baptized there in the church and began to be involved in different aspects of the ministry, working with children and driving a van for deaf and handicapped children. God gave me victory over many areas of my life—over cigarettes, over alcohol, over drugs—and gave me the desire to serve Him.

It was while I was there that I met Dr. Bob Jones Jr. for the first time. I had thought about going to Bob Jones University but didn't think I would be able to because of my background. I was a high school dropout and was on probation from the court system for a weapons violation, and I didn't think I would be the kind of student Bob Jones University would want to have. After talking to Dr. Bob, he said there was a possibility and that he would do whatever he could in order for me to be able to attend the University in the fall of 1974, which I did. I was able to get a General Equivalency Diploma that summer, and although I was still on probation from the court system, I went to the University. I had been accepted on academic probation because of my educational background. Yet the four years I spent at Bob Jones University were great years of enrichment and character building and of developing convictions. It was a great experience for me and one I look back on with great fondness. It was during my junior year at Bob Jones that I met my wife, who was a senior. We began to date and were married following my graduation from Bob Jones University.

I look back on what God allowed me to do there and the opportunities I had to serve Him. I was the sophomore and also the junior class chaplain. I was also the chaplain of our society, Epsilon Zeta Chi, for one semester. I was inducted into Who's Who in American Colleges and Universities and graduated from the University with honors, cum laude. As I look back I can see that God did it all. God took me from the streets of Philadelphia and enabled me to do what humanly would have been unthinkable.

After I got saved, my father went back to speak to many of those same men in prison he had seen and known through the years and told them, "My son has become a Christian." Then as time went on, he was able to share other news with them—"My son is a student at Bob Jones University. . . . My son is preparing for the ministry. . . . He is preparing for the mission field." We see how God worked through all that; and what a joy it was for my father to be able to go back and testify to the grace of God in the life of his son who was now converted and studying to be a preacher of the Word of God.

his son who was now converted and studying to be a preacher of the Word of God.

When I graduated from Bob Jones University in 1978, I felt the need for further education, not knowing if I would be going into the pastorate or into missions. I decided to go to Pennsylvania where my parents lived, where my brother was pastor of a church and where I could attend Calvary Baptist Theological Seminary. I finished seminary in 1982. At that time I went back to Philadelphia to plant a church, five minutes from where I was born. God gave us a rich ministry there where I started a new work and pastored for five years.

Even before going back to Philadelphia my first burden was for missions, and in seminary I thought that one day I would be on the mission field. I see why God kept us in Philadelphia. He enabled us to have some experience to prepare us for missions. In 1987, after being at the church for five years, I resigned from Faith Independent Baptist Church, and a friend of mine became pastor. My family and I went to France in order to help a Frenchman plant churches. We arrived in France in January 1988 and were there over six years. We were involved in starting two churches and teaching at the Bible Institute near Paris. While we lived in France, the Berlin Wall came down, and in the following years many changes took place. After the revolution in Romania in December 1989, there were a lot of opportunities for service in Eastern Europe, so I began to visit Romania and other Eastern European countries without a thought of leaving France. But in May of 1994, we moved to Romania, and God has given us a great ministry here. As we look back, we see that God prepared us step by step. He directed us to serve Him through various ministries.

8

No Sivnksty Had Ever Gone to College

No Sivnksty Had Ever Gone to College

JERRY SIVNKSTY (ATTENDED 1961-67)

One day in West Virginia one of my Roman Catholic cousins heard a knock on her door. She opened the door, and a man said, "I'm from a Baptist church, and I would like to come to talk with you." She said, "I'm a Roman Catholic." He said, "That makes no difference," and she said, "Come on in." So my cousin heard the Word of God from Pastor Doug Rutherford who was a Bob Jones graduate, and he led her to Jesus Christ. Well, when her husband came home that night, she told him what she had done. He went to church and heard the Word of God preached, and he also got saved.

Then they came to my house and invited me to go to church with them—now, of course I was a Roman Catholic. My cousin said, "Jerry, I would like to take you to church with me this coming Sunday." I thought we were going to a Catholic church, but I asked, "Where are we going to go?" I was told, "We are going to a Baptist church." I said, "Baptist church—what is that like?" He said, "Well, it is a little different from a Catholic church." (I want you to know there is *quite* a difference.)

Well, I got to this Baptist church, and everything was different. Everything bothered me until the man of God began to preach. When he began to preach, for the first time I heard that Jesus Christ died for my sins. I was greatly moved and stirred. When I got home, I told my mother, "Mom, you have got to go and hear this man preach. He preaches the Bible." My mother was a Roman Catholic, and she had never been in a Baptist church in her life. So the next Sunday my mother went to church with me and heard the Word of God preached, and she too was greatly touched. When we started going back home that day, my mother said to me, "Do you think we ought to go back to that Baptist church next Sunday?" I said, "Mom,

I think we ought to go back. What do you think?" She said, "Yes, let's go back."

The next Sunday a snowstorm hit in West Virginia. We had a terrible road because we lived way back in the country and got deep ruts in the road. My mother was driving the car through the snowstorm to this Baptist church, and she said to me, "Jerry, do you think I ought to go forward and get saved today?" Here I am. I am unsaved. I don't know the Bible, and I said, "Mom, I believe you ought to go forward and get saved today." And my mother got saved that day because of my encouragement. I was a soulwinner before the Lord even saved me.

The following Sunday my mother and I went back to church. I was under deep conviction, so I sat way in the back of the church, and my mother sat in the front part of the church. When the man gave the invitation, my mother turned around and looked at me and motioned with her hand for me to go forward, but I shook my head no. Mother got more furious and tried to encourage me to go forward, but I was so embarrassed and so shy that I would not go forward. But that night I prayed this prayer. I said, "Dear God, next Sunday I am going to go to church and get saved." Now, isn't that interesting? Here I was a religious person, and I realized I needed Christ as my Savior. The next Sunday I went to church, and that night I got saved. Then three months later my father, Mike Sivnksty, got saved. His life was greatly changed.

I was saved my senior year in high school, and when I graduated I had no intention of going to college because no Sivnksty had ever gone to college, and I was not going to be the first one. You see, while I was in high school my whole life was playing sports. I played football for three years and baseball for three years, and really I was an outdoorsman.

That summer after graduation I worked for a tree nursery, planting shrubbery, and my mother saw an advertisement in the paper that there was a job opening at the newspaper company, and the job was based upon who had the most words per minute on the typing test. So my mother said, "Jerry, you ought to go take that test." Well, I had worked in the ground with my hands all summer, and I said, "Mom, I can't type. I have been working in the ground all summer, and I couldn't do anything." But she kept after me and hounded me to go take that test, so just to get Mom off me, I said, "OK, Mother, I will go take that test." When I sat down and took the test at the typewriter, it seemed like my hands became limber, and they just flew across those keys. I was kind of shocked and surprised. Well, a couple of days later I got a phone call from the newspaper company saying, "Jerry, you had the most words per minute, so you get the job." So I worked for the *Fairmont Times* newspaper company in Fairmont, West Virginia.

While I was working one day, Pastor Doug Rutherford said, "Jerry, would you like to go down and visit a Christian school in Greenville, South Carolina, called Bob Jones University?" I said, "Well, yes, I would be interested in going down there." There were several of us young people going to go down. I had never heard of Bob Jones University, and there was a young man who was going to go with me whom I greatly admired. He was a tremendous Christian young man, I thought; so we got ready to go to Greenville, South Carolina, to visit this school. When we got in the car, this young man said to me, "Jerry, I am going to fast for the next two days going to Bob Jones University." I admired him and looked up to him a great deal, so I said, "I'm going to fast too." The problem was that I had never fasted in my entire life. I usually ate four or five meals a day. We got in the car and started going down the road. We stopped at a restaurant, and the pastor got out of the car and walked toward the restaurant. This young man and I stayed in the back seat, so the pastor came back and said to this young man, "Aren't you going to eat lunch?" Very piously the young man said, "I am fasting." He said, "What about you, Jerry?" I said, "No, sir, I am fasting also." Well, the pastor had a lovely meal and came back, and he rubbed in how good the meal was. We started going on down the road, and my stomach started growling so loud I was embarrassed. I saw these big cheeseburgers on the billboards and big bottles of Pepsi, and, man, I was dying. When we stopped for supper that night, again the pastor said to the young man, "Are you going to eat supper?" He replied, "No, I am fasting." "What about you, Jerry?" "No, sir, I am fasting also." Well, that night for the first time in my life I went to bed without any food in my body, and that entire night, I didn't count sheep, I counted cheeseburgers! I was dying for food.

The next morning when we got up, I really was hurting. We went to breakfast, and the pastor said to this young man, "Are you going to have breakfast?" "No, I am fasting." "What about you, Jerry?" "No, sir, I am fasting also." Well, my dear pastor friend had some good friends in Greenville, and we went to their home for lunch, and I mean this lady had a spread of food you wouldn't believe. She had a big bowl of mashed potatoes and sweetened tea, and she had biscuits and a big plate of meat, and by this time the pastor was really getting upset. The lady had to go in the house to get something, so the pastor turned to this young man and said, "Young man, are you going to eat lunch?" "No, sir, I am fasting." Then the pastor turned to me and said, "Jerry, are you going to eat lunch?" I said, "No, sir, I am fasting also." The pastor got so mad at me he said, "Now listen, Jerry, you are fasting because he is. Why don't you eat?" I said, "OK." Boy, did I ever eat. I learned a valuable lesson not to imitate people, especially in the area of fasting!

Because I fasted two days traveling to Greenville, everything went wrong. I was really weak and, therefore, just had a bad time. When I got in the car to leave Greenville, South Carolina (I will never forget this), I looked out the back window of the car and waved at the school and said out loud, "Bob Jones University, you will never see me again!" I am embarrassed I said those words, but I did it because of what had happened.

Shortly after this Pastor Rutherford said, "Jerry, could we send an application for you to go to Bob Jones?" I said, "Sure, go ahead, send it in." The reason I said this was that I had such terrible grades in high school that I knew I could not be accepted at any college. I am not proud of my terrible grades, but I did not study—I just played sports. So I knew there was no way any school was going to accept me, especially Bob Jones University.

I was coming home from work one day and was so happy. I was driving my nice truck. As I got near my house, I saw my cousin Mary Ann sitting on the front porch and waving a letter, and I got this "death" feeling in my stomach. I said, "Oh, no, I bet that is from Bob Jones University, and I bet they have accepted me." I got out of the truck, and my cousin said, "Jerry, it is from Bob Jones University." I said, "Give me the letter," and I grabbed it in disgust. I opened the letter, and sure enough, they had accepted me. Man, I got so discouraged. I didn't want to go to college. I was almost in a state of depression.

One day my pastor said, "Jerry, my family is having a picnic at Grafton Dam. Would you like to go along with us?" I said, "OK." He said, "Just meet me at Grafton at the park." I knew where it was, so I went home and took a shower and got in my truck and drove up to Grafton. As I got out of the truck, all the people from my church started coming out of the woods. They had been hidden, and in front of all these people, Pastor Doug Rutherford said, "Well, Jerry. This is a surprise going-away party for you." They had bought me clothes and all kinds of things for college, and then in front of all these people, Pastor said, "Well, Jerry, I guess you can't back out now, can you?"

It seemed like God forced me to go to Bob Jones University, but before I got there—between the time of the picnic and the time I went to school—God called me to preach. I heard a missionary from West Pakistan, Dr. Gene Gurganus, preach in our church; and as he gave the message, my heart was deeply stirred to give my life for the Lord's service. I wept as I walked down the aisle, and then I stood there in the front and told the Lord that I did not know how He could use me—mainly I thought because of my speech problems. However, I wanted to give Him my life and use it as He saw fit. My speech problems were primarily due to the foreign languages I was raised with and because of the harassment of other children in our area because we were foreigners to them. So once I got to school, I had all sorts of difficulties with speech. I am indebted to some speech teachers—Mr. Bob Pratt and Miss Joyce Parks—who really worked with me and helped, through phonics, to turn on a light in my mind so I could understand how to pronounce words. I am indebted to them because I believe that without them I would not have made it.

I have now traveled across the country in evangelism for twenty-five years, since 1970. I thank the Lord that my training was from this institution that helped shape and mold my life for the glory of the Lord.

9

Standing True

Standing True

D. R.

I was born on a farm in Arkansas in 1931 to a large family. I was the eleventh child in a family of thirteen children. Down the road there was a little Baptist church; I am sure that is the first place my mother and daddy ever took me. They attended regularly, and I went there with them until I was nineteen years old and went into the military.

In 1945 the church planned what the old-timers called a "protracted" meeting. Today we would call it a revival meeting or evangelistic meeting. They had torn down the old church building and were building a new church building. But it had not progressed as far as they had planned, so the men went out into the woods and cut down some poles and built a brush arbor. The fact is, some of the teenage boys, including me, helped them. They put sawdust on the ground. They brought the pews in and brought the piano in. They built a platform for preaching, and they had their revival meeting.

One night the preacher preached on hell, and he scared me out of it. I had always planned to be saved someday, but that night I realized that I really wasn't too smart if I refused Christ and ended up in hell. The night that I was saved under the brush arbor three other teenagers and a man and his wife were saved. Others were saved during the meeting. God gave a wonderful meeting. That was one of the last times they used a brush arbor in our community as I remember it.

Although I was saved at fourteen, I drifted away from the Lord during my high school years, but I came back to Him while I was in the navy. When the Lord called me to preach, I had been reading the *Sword of the Lord* for some time, so I wrote to Dr. John R. Rice and asked him about a Christian college I might attend. He said, "If you think you're going to be a pastor, it might be good to go to

Tennessee Temple. If you think God wants you to be an evangelist, it would be good to go to Greenville, South Carolina, and go to Bob Jones University and sit at the feet of Dr. Bob Jones Sr." I didn't feel impressed to go to either of the schools. I thought the Lord wanted me to go to a Baptist college in Arkansas.

I entered that college in the fall of 1955, and that fall the college decided to teach a dancing course for the girls. The preacher boys' class was against this—about 165 preacher boys—and they stood up against it; however, the faculty and administration said, "We are running the school for the Baptists in Arkansas; the preacher boys aren't."

One of the senior ministerial students said that he was pastoring a church, and he asked them what he could tell his young people when he preached against dancing and they stood up and said, "Well, Preacher, they're teaching it up there at the college where you go." They didn't answer him, and I don't think they could answer him.

It was during this "deal" about dancing that I went home one day for lunch. My wife and I lived in an apartment just off campus. My wife had been reading the Bob Jones University catalog, and she said to me, "You know, at Bob Jones University they won't even let the preacher boys smoke," and my response was, "Thank God there is someone someplace that stands for something." And I started in my heart right then to go to Bob Jones University.

My preacher-boy friends said, "If you go, the Baptists will put you in the back of the book. You won't be able to preach." Of course, that isn't true. I said, "Well, if that is what they are going to do, they may as well do it because that is what I am going to do. I am going to go to Bob Jones." In the fall of 1956, I entered Bob Jones University, and I will be eternally thankful to God that I did.

After getting out of school, graduating, I held some meetings and pastored some churches. In 1970 I was encouraged by an old preacher to go to a southern city and start an independent Baptist church. I told my wife what the old gentleman had said, and it seemed kind of funny to us. It seemed like something way out of the realm of anything we would ever do, but it kind of grew on me. We ended up going to a city he had suggested and, as some say, started from scratch—I say we started from itch! We didn't have any families, and no one had pledged to help us. We just rented a building and started visiting. I am sure there are a hundred different ways better than the way we did it, but God did bless and raised up a church. A number of people went out of that church to attend Bob Jones University.

After we bought land and built a building, we had a furnace put in. But we didn't have any gas. We were using makeshift construction site heaters—boiler, kerosene, whatever. It really wasn't acceptable, but the gentleman—bless his heart—who offered this was doing the best he could, and we were doing the best we could.

One Sunday evening in the public service I prayed and reminded the Lord that we had started that church as a soul-saving station to reach people for Christ and to train them for Him. In my prayer I admitted that it was a small thing with Him and a big thing with us, but if He'd be pleased, we would be grateful if He would let us have heat the next Sunday. My wife worked at a bank with a lady whose husband was a bona fide plumber, and he said, "Well, if you can get the gas company to run the gas line in there, I will hook it up to the furnace for you." So Monday morning I called the gas company, and they said, "Our crew is out of town this week. Should they get back in town in time on Friday, we will send them out and let them use the backhoe and lay the line up to the church." As it turned out, they did; on Saturday the plumber came by and connected the furnace, and the next Sunday morning we had heat.

Now God answered a lot of prayers in that work and in other works we have helped get started, but this stands out in my mind because some years later at Bob Jones University I ran into a girl who, along with her family, had attended that church. They were there the night we had the prayer, and she talked about someone back there who could pray and get the gas turned on. I thank God that a number of teenagers and young people were impressed with the fact that God does hear and answer prayer. The fact is, I was impressed myself that God does hear and answer our prayers.

Another thing that has happened to me since I left Bob Jones University is that God gave us four boys. The world says that if you spare the rod, you spoil the child. The Bible is always stronger than

71

the world. The Bible says in Proverbs 13 that if you spare the rod, you hate the son. That is a much stronger statement. I love my boys, and we borrowed the wisdom from the book of Proverbs to raise them for Christ. All of them are saved; all of them are in some type of service for the Lord. One of them is a missionary, and one of them is still in training, and I thank God for giving those boys to us and for the opportunity to raise them for Him. They all four have attended Bob Jones University. Three of them have master's degrees from the school. I thank God for the day my wife reminded me about a place where they took a stand for something, and my prayer is that the school will always stand true because there might be a boy or a girl someday that needs someplace to go.

10

God's Special Place

God's Special Place

ROMULO WEDEN RIBEIRO (ATTENDED 1988-92)

I was born on October 17, 1964, in a small city in the midwest of Brazil. I am the fourth of six children in the family. A few months before I was born, my parents professed faith in the Lord Jesus Christ, but, unfortunately, they did not take their decision seriously and did not become real Christians for a long time.

I was seven years old when I received my first impression of God. Both of my parents worked full time in a bar, leaving us children unattended during the day. One morning I was crossing a busy avenue with other children when a car traveling forty-five miles per hour hit me. I was immediately taken to the hospital. The driver thought he had killed me because I was disfigured and could not move. In spite of my appearance, none of my bones were broken, and the wounds were only superficial. When my parents came to pick me up at the hospital, I overheard my unsaved mother saying to my father, "When I woke up this morning, I did not know why, but I felt I needed to pray for God's protection over my children today." I knew then that God had spared my life. That day, I started praying to God, although I did not have knowledge of the gospel or of the Savior.

About that time, my parents started having serious marital problems, and they finally separated when I was nine. My mother continued working at that same bar, and my father took three of us with him to the south of the country. There he bought another bar in order to support us. While I was still a child, I helped him sell alcoholic beverages to the customers. I used to idolize most of those customers, and I could hardly wait for the day that I could drink just like them. My mother started having emotional problems which caused her to lose her job, and over a period of seven years, she was hospitalized thirty-eight times.

By God's providence, my father met an American missionary, Jimmy Rose (a BJU graduate), who witnessed to him and tried to bring him back to the Lord. One day Jimmy Rose went to see my father at the bar. When he saw me, a twelve-year-old child, selling liquor, he told my father that he had to get rid of the bar in order to serve God and save his own son from an anguishing future. My father accepted the challenge and sold the bar as soon as possible and became a salesclerk in a clothing store. He went to church and became very active, and I followed his steps soon after, receiving the Lord Jesus as my personal Savior.

We had severe financial problems after my father sold the bar. At first, I was very embarrassed to go to church because of our poverty. For months I went to church in an old pair of pants with a broken zipper which was fastened with a paper clip. My only shirt was faded and twice my size. My shoes had two big holes on each sole. Often I felt a great desire to go to the altar to pray during the invitation but did not because I was afraid that people would see the holes in my shoes or, worse yet, that the paper clip would come undone. I used to walk about seven miles every day going to and from school because we could not afford bus tickets. We started having a lack of food as well. On a certain day I had had neither breakfast nor lunch, and as I walked home from school, I found fifty cents on the street. I passed by a bakery and bought a *paozinho,* a small loaf of French bread. When I arrived home, I found that my older sister had not eaten either. I gave her my bread, lying by saying that I had already eaten at school.

As a consequence of our financial problems, my father delayed the payments of our rent for three months. The owner of the house, along with three other men, threatened my father physically, giving him only three more days to leave the house. For the first time in my life I saw my father crying because he had been humiliated and was not able to provide for his family. This all happened shortly after our conversion. My father and I started praying for a miracle. The church does not know to this day what we went through those first days. But a miracle happened to strengthen our faith in the Lord Jesus Christ. On the third day, the last day before we had to leave the house, a lady who worked at the same store as my father gave him the key to her unoccupied house and told him he did not have to pay rent until the following month. When my father arrived home with that key in his hands, I jumped up and down on my bed and shouted many amens to the glory of God. The Lord was only testing us, and the suffering prepared us for the spiritual victories which God was about to pour upon our lives.

About that time, I started working at my first job. I started studying in the evening and working forty-five hours per week cleaning cars at an automobile shop. I grew spiritually at my workplace because of persecution and also because of the many opportunities I had to witness there. My first week of work was not that great. I punched a young man's nose because he came behind me making obscene gestures because I was a Christian. My boss did not fire me but started persecuting me as well. I had planned to buy a new pair of pants and a pair of shoes when I received my first paycheck, but the money was not enough. However, my father reminded me that I needed to pay my tithe, which I did. After one year at that job, I was promoted and my salary increased five times. I had enough money to give to my father and to the church and to spend on myself.

At the time we got saved, my parents had been separated for almost four years. From day one of my salvation, I started praying that my mother would come back to my father. When I would ask him if he was willing to forgive her, the answer was always negative, but I knew that God could change his heart as well as hers. I prayed persistently every day, and after five years, God finally fulfilled the desire of my heart. When I was seventeen, my mother showed up without any warning, telling us that she had received the Lord Jesus as her personal Savior through the influence of two godly ladies God had put in her life. She learned from those ladies that in order to get right with God she needed to return to her family. People who see my parents today cannot imagine they ever had serious marital problems. That same year, I met the one who would become my wife, Rachel Joy, daughter of Thomas and Linda Gilmer, missionaries to the Jews in Brazil. Rachel was born and raised in Brazil.

God gave me a wonderful local church through which I was able to grow toward Christlikeness. I graduated from our Bible Institute in 1986. Also in 1986, through the recommendation of my pastor, Jimmy Rose, Dr. Bob Jones III invited me to come to Bob Jones University as a Timothy student. Before I could be enrolled I had to overcome three big obstacles: I had to learn English, pass an English test (TOEFL), and get my student visa. I failed the English exam twice, and the American consulate would not give me a student visa until I passed the test. In the opinion of many good Christians, the obstacles were a sign from God that it was not His will for me to go to BJU. They believed I needed no further training for the ministry. I realized Satan was trying to prevent me from going to Bob Jones University.

I finally secured a temporary student visa. Two weeks before my departure, while I was driving the church's van, I hit a motorcyclist who seemed to have appeared out of nowhere. He was badly injured. I took him immediately to the hospital. In the deepest part of my heart, I could feel the presence of the Holy Spirit comforting me, though I did think that this was the end of my hope of going to BJU. Fortunately, an eyewitness I had never met before testified for me in court, stating that the motorcyclist had cut sharply in front of me. The following day I went to visit this motorcyclist and had the opportunity to witness to him.

The week of my departure, my mother became very ill and was hospitalized. I was willing to stay in Brazil if her doctor and my father thought it would be necessary, but they promised me she would get well. In the airplane going to the States, someone stole my wallet with my documents and three hundred dollars cash. Fortunately, my passport and traveler's checks were in my front pocket. When I arrived at my destination, Greenville, South Carolina, I had only two dollars in my pocket.

Finally, in the fall of 1988, after taking the TOEFL exam for the third time, I entered Bob Jones University as a full-time student. God used two phrases to confirm His will for me at that time: "BJU—God's special place for you" and "BJU—The Opportunity Place." Once in the dorm, I did not have money for laundry and for personal hygiene items. One day after praying by myself in Portuguese at a time when I knew my roommates were in class, I found an envelope with my name misspelled on it. There was a five-dollar bill which enabled me to do my laundry and to buy a few other things. I felt as if I were in a little piece of heaven.

For a few months I could not understand the announcements made in chapel, which caused me to receive a few demerits. Although my English was very marginal, I was able to succeed in my first semester at BJU because of my teachers' willingness to help me. That first semester and part of the second semester as well, I would get up at 5:30 almost every morning to study. I realized my English was getting better when I finally understood an entire message by Dr. Bob Jones Jr.—one on salvation. Tears came down my face that day.

When the cold weather arrived, my roommates helped me find heavy clothes in the dorm's mission barrel. I spent my first Christmas in the States at BJU, working in the Dining Common during the day and working as a security guard during the night. It was wonderful! I really miss those days because I got very close to God. Also, the money I made during Christmas was enough to supply all my personal needs during the following semester.

During my second semester at BJU, I was invited to travel with Dr. Bob Jones III as a Timothy student. I felt like Mephibosheth when he was invited by King David to eat bread at his table. Spending a whole day with Dr. Bob and other faculty members was a wonderful opportunity for me. Before I went to BJU, some people at my home church warned me not to become proud or arrogant since I was going to the best Christian school in the world. I wrote back to my church and said it was impossible to become proud and arrogant when the president of the school and the teachers were so humble themselves.

I got married the summer before my junior year. My wife, Rachel, started working in the Records Office at Bob Jones University, and the school had a great spiritual impact on her life.

Ever since my first semester at BJU, I had a purpose in my heart—to bring my father from Brazil for my graduation. Once again, God fulfilled the desire of my heart. I was able to save some money throughout my four years of college which I used to pay for my father's ticket to the United States. He not only witnessed my graduation but also heard me preach in the finals of the annual sermon contest and was with me when my little daughter, Rochelle, was born just three days after Commencement. My father had sold his sinful business. In exchange God gave him a son in the ministry; God brought his wife back to him; and best of all, God gave him the peace that belongs only to those who do His perfect will.

May the Lord bless my father, my pastor, my local church, Dr. Bob Jones III, Bob Jones University, and many other Christians for making possible the blessing of God in my life.

11

By the Grace of God

By the Grace of God

PAUL HANTZ BERNARD (ATTENDED 1984-90)

The day of my graduation from Bob Jones University, May 7, 1988, I took the bulletin of the Commencement activities and wrote on it: "By the grace of God, I am what I am." A simple statement, isn't it? Yet God and I knew how deeply in my life its roots imbibed that inspiration.

The festivities were under way, but my thoughts had already migrated back to Haiti, to that little town where I was born. When I was only five, my mother, unable to cope with the financial demands of rearing me, took me to my uncle, my father's brother. I lived with him until he passed away fourteen years later. For most of those years I craved parental affection and searched for my own identity, trying to anchor my life to things and people which proved as temporal as the fragrance of perfume left behind by a passerby. They were years of questioning the unfair inequalities of life, years of presumption to prove to that hostile world that "I am somebody," years of pain, years of bittersweet discoveries, years which culminated in my meeting two missionary ladies.

As I was thus reflecting on my past, someone announced that the graduates should stand. I suddenly returned to reality—both the reality of the ceremony and the reality of how the events of my life prepared me for this memorable moment.

The routine of watching diplomas being given to the graduates eased my return to the film of my life. It was on a hot Friday afternoon back in the mid-'70s that the two missionaries met me. I was practicing soccer alone on a field neighboring my house. Why was I out there alone in the heat? Well, God's grace was at work. The ladies invited me to a youth club they had just begun not far from my house. Some time later I accompanied some friends to the youth group. Drawn by the kind attention I received there, I continued visiting regularly, bringing with me my load of cravings, searchings, questionings, and sufferings. I became active and was, consequently, confronted with the gospel. On a Friday evening in October 1978, one of the two ladies led me to the Lord. My burdens ("and You know, Lord, how heavy and how many they are," I said in my prayer that evening), yes, my burdens rolled away. I remember feeling literally very light as I walked back home. You see, God's grace is a saving grace!

Again I "awoke," as a student gave his testimony at the microphone set up for that purpose. How gracious the Lord had been toward him also. I was able to relate to him, remembering how I progressed in the club. I became one of the leaders and finally the president of the group. I taught, preached, participated in the organization and leadership of camps, and became a leader in the church I had joined. Why was I so much involved? Why did I enjoy it so? At first I desired to become a Roman Catholic priest so that, as I thought in my naiveté, I might change the Roman Church. The grace of God had other plans. One evening God activated the flickering flame of service in my heart. It became a fire that inflamed my life. During a Bible study class, I inadvertently turned to I Corinthians 9:23, "And this I do for the gospel's sake, that I might be partaker thereof," instead of the passage announced by the teacher. That was it! It was clear that God's grace is a calling grace. How refreshing it is to say with Paul, "Unto me, who am less than the least of all saints, is this grace given, that I should preach . . . the unsearchable riches of Christ" (Eph. 3:8).

Oh, yes! The graduation ceremony! The School of Religion graduates were now being introduced. Filled with various emotions, I stood as a prospective recipient of a B.A. in pastoral studies with a minor in publishing. So many years and events separated this moment from that "inadvertent" turn to I Corinthians 9:23. But was it really inadvertent? Or was it God's grace at work? It was no more inadvertent to turn to I Corinthians 9:23 than to turn, ever since that evening, to a new course of life—a course studded with obstacles and blessings. Had I taken the time to assess the obstacles, I might have abdicated the right to the crown of full-time service to the Lord. Had I counted the blessings beforehand, I might have been covetous and served with the wrong motive.

Many questions crossed my mind then. What will my strongly Roman Catholic family say? What will my uncle say—he who wanted me to replace him as a lawyer? What would my father say—he who wanted me to become a medical doctor? Where would I study? How would I pay? The months were passing. The awareness of my calling was intensifying. The reality of the obstacles was becoming clearer. Meanwhile, my uncle passed away, and I moved to the home of a sister who herself was struggling to survive because her husband had left her.

One day an American pastor visited the youth club. He had come to investigate the field with his daughter, then a prospective missionary and a new graduate of Bob Jones University. He talked to the missionary ladies and me about the Timothy program and promised to recommend me as soon as he returned to the United States. He kept his promise, and soon I received an application form from the Admissions Office. Now I had to master English, calm the fear of some missionaries who thought I might not come back, persuade the officials at the American embassy that, indeed, I was going to attend BJU. The Lord smoothed the process. When I went to the embassy, the consul looked at my dark skin and exclaimed, "You at Bob Jones?" He called another official and made some remarks while pointing his finger toward me. Then they both laughed! That happened just after the court case which contributed to the world's negative and unfair stereotype of the school. For one reason or another, maybe to enjoy the fun even more, the consul granted me the visa. Or perhaps it was because God's grace is an assisting grace?

On July 27, 1984, I left Haiti and spent five weeks with a pastor in Palm Harbor, Florida. He and his people received me graciously. That sojourn started a mutual friendship which still endures. During that time, I watched television nearly all day long in order to perfect my hearing the English language. Consequently, when I began classes that fall, I never needed to record the lectures on tape as some foreign students have to do. Yet I was not perfect. In spite of my faithfulness to the unusual rules, adaptation to the unusual culture, and ease in the unusual language, some failure occurred. I remember how I turned "purple," fearing I would be expelled unjustly for breaking the rule about no physical contact with the opposite sex. Indeed, one day in response to a joke of mine, a girl told me, "You are pulling my leg!"

Yet, realizing the privilege granted to me, I decided to make the most of it. One Haitian proverb I repeated often to myself was this: I came to drink milk, not to count cows. (That is, I came to take advantage of the opportunities but not to mingle in things which are none of my business.) And "milk" I drank! Throughout my undergraduate years (except for the first semester), God's grace enabling me, I worked twenty hours a week and carried a twenty-hour academic load each semester. My goal was to save money for graduate school and to have a head start by taking some graduate courses during my undergraduate years. My strength resided in my waking up at 5:30, the earliest I was allowed, to spend time with the Lord. The results were evident. Classes! I graduated cum laude. Soccer! During all four years I made the all-star team as the best fullback. Contests! I won the sermon contest my junior year, having been an alternate my sophomore year. Leadership! I became society chaplain my junior year and ministerial class president my senior year. Honors! I was selected for Who's Who in American Colleges and Universities and also for Christian leadership.

Does all that listing insinuate a flicker of pride? If so, I have made my point. By my senior year I had lost the reality that all those blessings had been granted to me by the enabling grace of God. I thought I had been doing it on my own, and I paid for it. I soon discovered, thank God, that His grace was also a chastising grace. Indeed, it became evident to me that something was withholding God's blessings. I had lost the taste and strength for the 5:30 prayer times. I even became weak in soccer. The day before I had to make an important trip with Dr. Bob Jones III, I had an accident which could have taken my life. The Lord withheld so many blessings from me that it was at times distasteful to think about my being in the ministry. Our greatest blessings may be either our greatest temptation or our greatest opportunity of service. It all depends to which one we will let God's grace lead us. Is it not God's grace that we can recognize His chastising hand in our lives? Woe to the one who is chastised and who does not even know it—or worse, who knows it and does not learn from it. Those bitter experiences stand today as an angel "of Satan to buffet me"—to keep me from exalting myself! For when I am weak, then I am strong.

By now, the line of students was moving slowly toward the stage where Dr. Bob Jones III was handing the diploma folders to the graduates. I thought then, "If he knew of me what God and I know, would he still give me that diploma?" Oh, how discreet God's grace can be in some areas of our lives!

Amidst all the disciplining, the Lord, in His pardoning grace, extended to me an invitation through Bibles International to pursue special studies in view of becoming a Bible translator. It then became clear to me why, ever since my freshman year, I had been saving money for graduate school—well, more accurately, for the first semester of graduate school, for that was as far as my savings took me.

Graduation was a sign that the University had fulfilled its contract toward me for the Timothy program. What about graduate school? It was as if God's grace were whispering in my ear, "If you are so great, go ahead and do it alone!" I refused. I had already had my own Peniel experience (Gen. 32). I was limping from the blows in my spiritual thigh (and still am). No more of such a fight! And the Lord blessed me.

Where would I live? I had prayed that the Lord would open the door of a specific Christian home for me to remain there during my graduate years. He did! One evening the phone of my dorm room rang. It was the father. He said, "Hantz, we cannot help you as much as we would like to, but if you desire to live with us, you are welcome." But they lived far from the school, so what would I drive? I prayed the Lord that He would also be gracious to provide a car. He was, and a car was given to me.

The first summer after graduation I attended summer school full time, still working twenty hours a week. But by fall, my four-year savings were about gone. The Lord entreated me not to ask help from anyone but to work hard and trust Him for the rest. His faithfulness proved itself graciously. On many occasions I received anonymous gifts of five hundred or a thousand dollars or even more. I felt bad to be receiving so much. Since my student visa did not allow me to work more than twenty hours while attending school and did not allow me to work for any employer other than the University, I applied for a work permit. Immigration said, "No!" It was as if God's grace were telling me, "Now to him that worketh is the reward not reckoned of grace, but of debt. But to him that worketh not, but believeth on him that justifieth the ungodly, his faith is counted for righteousness" (Rom. 4:4-5). Notwithstanding the amount of theology packed in those words, they reflected well my experience; that is, it was all by grace. And so it went throughout graduate school. In two years I completed the requirements for the Master of Divinity program, coupled with a summer of linguistics.

This time when Dr. Bob Jones III handed me the diploma folder on graduation day, he said, "You are among those who deserve it most." And I thought, "I'd better not let that go to my head!" How merciful God had been in His grace!

I went back to Haiti, limping on my "spiritual thigh." Throughout the past years, the Lord has opened the doors for me to launch and work on a Bible translation project, pastor a church, teach at a Bible seminary, and get involved in other occasional ministries. Amidst trials and blessings, He has held me close to Him. He has blessed me with a good wife and a wonderful family. Certainly, His grace is sufficient for me. Each time I fail in something, I feel I have received what I deserve. And if I succeed in something, I ask God to frame my heart like John Bunyan's. After delivering a fiery message at his parish, Bunyan was descending the steps from the platform when a lady told him, "Pastor, it was a wonderful message!" Bunyan answered quietly, "Thank you! The Devil already told me that as I was leaving the pulpit."

Today when I peruse the pages of the album containing my 1988 graduation pictures, I usually stop at the first page and sigh while I gaze at the cover of a bulletin of Commencement activities dated May 7, 1988, and on which this handwritten phrase can be read: "By the grace of God, I am what I am." May it always be so. Amen!

12

An Application for What?

An Application for What?

ROBERT E. VICKROY (ATTENDED 1961-66)

When I was six months old, my father was killed in a logging accident. My mother had to raise six children with virtually no means of income. I suppose the only means of income that she had at that time was what she received from the state of Michigan through the Aid for Dependent Children program. By the way, none of my brothers or sisters ended up as second-generation welfare recipients.

My mother died when I was eleven years old. I then went to live with my brother John, who had turned Roman Catholic when he married his wife. I lived with him for about a year and then went to live with my oldest sister. My sister had a son who was ten months older than I, and in the year that I turned sixteen, my brother-in-law gave an unusual Christmas present to his son and to me. He gave us a bottle of whiskey. My nephew and I thought we were really grown up because we could now drink just like the big boys. Very frankly, I am ashamed to say that on that Christmas Eve I drank too much of that bottle of whiskey and because of its influence got into a fight with my brother-in-law, which ended my stay at his home. I then went to live with another brother.

The following New Year's Day, my oldest brother, L.V., invited me to attend church with him. It was on that day, New Year's Day, that I trusted Jesus Christ as my personal Savior. Now, I have witnessed to my nephew and preached the gospel to my nephew many times, but he has refused to turn to Jesus Christ. Today he is still a drunk. Every time I see him, I praise the Lord that Jesus Christ saved my soul and that He also saved my life. I can truly testify every time I see him, "except for the grace of God . . ."

I graduated from high school in 1959. My brother John wanted so much for me to attend college. He said he did not want me to end up doing the same task he had done all of his life—working in

91

the laundry for Dow Chemical. So he had arranged for me to go to Denver, Colorado, to live with my brother Don and to attend Denver University. After we arrived in Denver (my brother John was going to stay there for a two-week vacation), almost immediately my brother Don arranged for me to go to work at the same place of business where he worked. While John and I were there, I had a compelling desire to return to Michigan. I did not want to stay in Colorado and attend Denver University. This overwhelming compulsion was in my heart for days, so when John was about ready to leave and return to Michigan, I told him that I wanted to go back to Michigan too. There was no argument. He simply said, "All right, that is what you can do." I was out of fellowship with the Lord at the time. I did not know at that time what caused this overwhelming compulsion; of course, I now know that it was God working in my heart and life even though I was out of fellowship with Him.

I returned to Michigan, and it was in September that the youth director of Byron Baptist Church had a mini-retreat for the teenagers at Meyers Lake. As the message was preached and encouragement was given to young people to dedicate themselves to live for Christ in the public school (of course, I was not returning to school that year), I rededicated my life to the Lord and determined by God's grace that I would be what God would have me to be.

When I was eighteen years of age, God began to impress upon me that I should become a preacher of the gospel. I would hear an evangelist preach, and the thought would come into my mind, "You should be a preacher." I would listen to Pastor Balcom, the pastor of Byron Baptist Church, preach the Word of God, and a still small voice would say within me, "You should become a minister of the gospel." But with my background, I thought I was mistaken. I thought I was just misreading what God was doing in my life. Certainly God would not call someone like me. I had rededicated my life to the Lord, and I told Him I wanted to be used of Him and would be willing to be whatever He wanted me to be, but I did not think that God could call me to preach.

Byron Baptist Church, my home church, was involved in a monthly singspiration with a number of other churches—something that would be almost impossible today. Churches just do not cooperate too much. After the Sunday night service was over, we would go to the selected church for a time of singing and a challenge from the Word of God. On the Sunday night I answered God's call to preach, the singspiration was held at Antrim Baptist Church in Byron, Michigan. When the service at our church ended, Barbara (who is now my wife of thirty-three years) and I, with another couple, went out to my car only to discover that the car had a flat tire. The tire was a skin—that is, it had no tread on the tire. In fact, the cords of the tire were visible. I thought we probably should not go because we would be late, but because of the persuasion of Barbara and the other couple, I quickly changed the tire and put on one of equal quality to the one that was flat, and off we went several miles over gravel road.

When we arrived at Antrim Baptist Church for the singspiration, the singing was finished, and the preacher, a visiting missionary, was giving the challenge. The only seats available to us were located behind a pillar that held up the church roof. In order to see the speaker, I had to lean over and look around that pillar. As I did so, that missionary preacher said these words, "Some of you have been waiting for a special revelation from God to answer His call for you to preach. You have been waiting for God to write your name across the sky and to say, 'I want you to preach,' when He has already said in His Word, 'Go ye into all the world, and preach the gospel to every creature'" (Mark 16:15). On the way home that night I shared with Barbara what was happening in my life. I shared with her what the missionary had said and how I believed that God was speaking to me about being a minister of the gospel. Barbara suggested that I talk with Pastor Balcom. On the following Sunday when I shared with Pastor Balcom what God was doing in my life and that I believed He wanted me to be a preacher, he simply said to me, "I want you to come down to my office in the morning, and I will help you fill out an application." My response was, "An application for what?" He said, "An application for college. Also, bring ten dollars with you." That was the application fee for admission to Bob Jones University at the time. The next day as I sat in Pastor Balcom's office and answered questions that were on the application, he typed them in on an old Underwood manual typewriter.

I did not even pray about where I should go to college. I simply followed the leadership of my pastor. Certainly I do not think that is a wise thing for any young person—not to pray about where he ought to go to college—because it is such an important decision. But being an immature Christian and not knowing how to pray or what to do, I simply followed the leadership of my pastor. I am absolutely sure—just as sure as I am alive today—that it was God's will for me to attend BJU. It has also made me realize the importance of a pastor's influence. In a little over two years, Pastor Balcom sent sixteen young people from our small congregation to Bob Jones University. When I told my home church that I believed God had called me to preach, I think the only ones who really believed that God was speaking to me about the ministry were Pastor Balcom and Barbara.

After mailing the application, I received a packet from Bob Jones University, including a number of letters. One of the letters was from Dr. Bob Jones Sr., and in that letter he said, "Now that you have decided that God wants you to come to Bob Jones University, the Devil is going to do everything he can to fight your decision. He will even use good people to try to persuade you to go somewhere else to college." Shortly before I was to attend Bob Jones University, an elderly man at Byron Baptist Church said to me, "Why are you going so far away to go to college? We have our own school here in this state. You ought to attend this school." Just as sure as I am giving this testimony, I believe it was God's will for me to be at Bob Jones University, and Dr. Bob's letter protected me from being dissuaded from following what I now know to have been God's will.

After graduating from Bob Jones University, I went to Stanzel, Iowa, to pastor Bethel Baptist Church. I was there only a year. I did not know much about the ministry when I first began pastoring. I did not know the questions to ask. When I went to Stanzel, they were involved in a tent crusade every summer. Included in that tent crusade was one church identified with the National Council of Churches, and the evangelist that had been invited to speak at that tent meeting was an associate of Dr. Paul Smith, the pastor of the People's Church in Toronto, Canada. Because I learned that this man was a New Evangelical and because of the NCC connection, I made up my mind that Bethel Baptist Church could have nothing to do with that tent meeting.

As a young man, twenty-five years old, I went to the committee meeting for this tent revival and tried to explain as simply as I could why we ought not have the National Council church or the Four-square Gospel Church involved. I sat before some men—some preachers as well as deacons in the churches—who were fifty to sixty years old, men who should have been teaching me. As I told them what the Word of God said on separation, they seemed totally astonished that this was even in the Bible. Well, I said that Bethel Baptist Church would not cooperate with the meeting.

Normally the churches would close down their Sunday night service and their Wednesday night prayer meeting and go to the tent meeting, but I told our congregation that we would not do so. There were only two people who showed up for the Sunday night service besides my wife and Teresa, our oldest daughter. I preached just as if the rest of the congregation were there. This elderly couple came up to me after the service and said, "Pastor Vickroy, we want you to know that we believe that you are right." I got up shortly thereafter and read my resignation and had no idea where I was going to go.

God opened the door for me to pastor in Pennsylvania, and I pastored Calvary Gospel Church. Shortly after I began pastoring, we changed the name to Calvary Baptist Church. God blessed our ministry there. We saw the church renovated and our church attendance go from an average of 45 to 50 in Sunday school to an average of 120 in Sunday school. I was there six and a half years. Then God led us to Calvary Bible Church in Dowagiac, Michigan, where we have been for over twenty years.

13

*From the Reformatory
to Revival Meetings*

From the Reformatory to Revival Meetings

JIMMY ROSE (ATTENDED 1958-61)

I was born in Denver, Colorado, in 1937. My dad and mother were unsaved, and my dad was a drunkard. When I was seven years of age, they divorced. Many times I remember having to call somebody, even the police, to keep my dad from hurting my mother.

I was born and grew up in a very poor neighborhood. It was a neighborhood made up mainly of Mexican people and blacks. I grew up with young fellows who were dangerous. One young man was nicknamed Shuffles because he could dance well. He was a deadly young man, but he was one of my best friends at that time. How many times I thought, "One of these days I am going to get in trouble with this fellow, and he is going to kill somebody." He always wanted a gun and was always talking to somebody about where he could get a gun.

At an early age I was taken into one of the gangs called "The Heads." We learned several things in that gang, including how to make a zip gun from a car antenna. In the middle of my billfold I carried brass knuckles. If the police were to stop you and pass their hand over your billfold, they could not feel the brass knuckles. While I was still a young fellow, I was involved in gang fights. I am ashamed of those gang fights that I was in. I remember one time fourteen of us jumped on two young fellows. I did not participate much in that, but fourteen young men beat those two young fellows until their faces were red and bleeding. I was afraid they would really be hurt. In another fight I remember another one of my friends turning around and hitting a young man, and when he hit him, he broke his fist. He screamed out an oath and tried to kick him. He just missed kicking him in the face.

As just a young teenager, in one year I was arrested seven times. I had a certain innocent look about me, and every time I went before the judge, he kept giving me a chance. He thought there was some good in me and that I just needed to get with the right crowd so I would not be taken up with crime. He gave me chance after chance. I remember the time we were most scared. We had stolen a car in Denver, Colorado, and had driven to Colorado Springs. We were stopped by the police in Colorado Springs, and a nervous policeman stood there with a revolver. As we got out of the car, his floodlights were on us. As I looked up, I saw his revolver pointed at my head. It was a time of real fear. We were placed in jail in separate cells. It was Christmastime, and I will never forget the loneliness of that cell. I do not even remember there being a bed. I lay there on that cell floor and cried. It did not have to be that way, but I did not know the Lord Jesus Christ and did not know anything else.

Once again the judge was lenient and gave me a state leave. A state leave is where you are sent to another state. I was sent to Whitmire, South Carolina, where my half brother lived. I was to live with him. One more time I was a failure. I was involved in a car theft and breaking-and-entering and was placed in the county jail there in Whitmire. They had very little mercy, and in that county jail I stayed one month waiting to go before the judge for him to decide what to do with me.

They sent me back to Denver, Colorado, and I was placed in custody there. My probation officer thought that somehow I had changed. I had to a degree. I really did not want anything else to do with crime. I had even made a profession of faith in Whitmire, South Carolina, but time proved that it was not a real conversion. I stood before the judge one more time, and the probation officer said, "We have no recommendation for this young man. The only thing I can say is that it looks as if he has changed." Once again this judge gave me another chance. I was free but still on probation.

By this time my stepbrother had gotten out of the penitentiary, and I entered with him into crime—fighting and gang fighting and so forth. One night we were attempting to crack a safe. I was standing at the window as the lookout, and three others were trying to crack this safe. Although we did not know it, the alarm went off downtown at the police station. Of course, we didn't hear it. I saw one patrol car pass, and then all of a sudden it turned around and came back. I saw another one and another one. I screamed to the other three that the police were there, and we ran out the door. We split up and ran different ways. There was a fellow behind me named Jerry Martinez, a Mexican boy. He jumped the fence, and all of a sudden I bowed down beside the fence in the darkness of the night; the policeman went right over me and jumped the fence and caught Jerry Martinez. I heard the policemen kicking him. I heard Jerry scream, "Don't kick me again. Don't hit me again." As I stayed there bowed down, I was praying that they would not find me. I heard one of the policemen say, "There is another one around here somewhere." He shined his flashlight over the fence, picked me up by the nape of my neck, and took me in.

I went before the judge again. This time he did not even lift his eyes. The probation officer made absolutely no remarks. He said, "I sentence you to the state reformatory in Golden, Colorado, for an indefinite term." An indefinite term means you need to work your way out. You get out after you have earned so many points, and you can earn points by being comported, by not getting into trouble, and so on. By the time I had been there six months, I did not have a single point. I was in the hole all the time.

We tried to escape from the Golden State Reformatory three times. The first time was a rather foolish attempt to escape. They were taking those in our dormitory to see a movie that night, and three of us just broke line and ran. They had some college students working with the reformatory, and they ran after us; in no time we were caught and taken back. When you escaped from the Golden State Reformatory, it was a kind of disgrace for the guard who was over you at that time. I remember that guard putting me on a table and hitting me in the face with his fist time after time. That was to try to scare me never to do it again.

The second time we tried to escape, we thought we had it a little better planned. They were calling the Protestant young men out to go to church, and the Catholics were staying in the dining common where we were eating. As they called our names, three of us dropped down behind a brick wall and went out through the door and through the corral. The only thing was that there was a teacher who was late coming for lunch. He saw us, and I remember running across the field asking one of the fellows who was with me, "Chief, is there any chance that we can make it?" We saw them getting in a car and riding up over the pasture. He said, "If we can get to that mountain, they cannot come up that mountain in a car." As we ran, I looked back. A guard had gotten out of the car and run down one of the young men and knocked him down. I heard him hitting him. Then they caught me. Chief somehow got away and was caught later on. Again I was beaten with fists and open hands.

We planned well our last attempt to escape from the Golden State Reformatory. We had seen one of the young inmates cleaning the windows in our dormitory, so we saved some money and paid him to leave the bars unlocked. From down on the ground you could not see that the bars were unlocked on the second floor where we slept. We waited until we had a new guard. We were downstairs with the new guard, and the three of us told him that it was our responsibility to go up and clean up the dormitories. He was doubtful about it, but we went upstairs anyway. We knocked the block off the window and raised it, and the bars were open. We jumped from the second floor and ran out toward the barbed wire fence. How we ever got over that fence I will never know, but we got over it. We were starting up Lookout Mountain when they discovered that we had broken out. We looked back down on the reformatory, and lights were going around and around everywhere and sirens were being activated. We knew we were safe to a degree. The only way they could get up that mountain was on horseback. As we were going all night long to Denver, we had to cross a highway. We were lying down in high grass and could hear some of the guards telling people in a house not far away to be on the lookout because some boys had broken out of the state reformatory. They had the dogs with them, and I do not know why they did not smell where we were.

We got into Denver early in the morning and sneaked over to a friend's house. He got us some clothes and some money. We went to a picture show, and from there I called my mother who worked in a dry cleaner's. She was surprised. I told her I had broken out of the state reformatory and that I needed help. After work she immediately went to the bus station and bought a ticket to Oakland, California. I had to go home to get some clothes. I will never forget going out. I knew the police would be watching my home, but I knew a way in where I would go through a back alley and cut up another alley and go in through the back of my house. There I got some clothes and a suitcase packed. Here I was, just a fifteen- or sixteen-year-old boy. I caught the bus for Oakland, California. I had an uncle in Oakland; I was going there.

I got into Oakland and was not there very long when my mother called me. She was crying and said that my stepfather was going to turn me in to the police and tell them where I was, so she sent me another ticket to Greenville, South Carolina. Imagine what the Lord did. I can never remember having a clear presentation of the gospel given to me, but here God was working it out to bring me to the "Bible Belt," of all the places in the world. Bless the Lord for that. My dad, of course, was divorced from my mother, and he lived in Greenville. I worked. I was not getting into any trouble, but during this time, I always had that uneasy feeling that somehow the police were going to put their hand on my shoulder and say, "You have got to go back and finish your time and do even more time."

So I told my dad I wanted to join the army. I was only sixteen. You had to be seventeen with one of your parents' consent. So I joined the Army Airborne. My dad signed for me, and, of course, there was no criminal record brought up in Greenville, South Carolina. I served my basic training and then some more. I received a furlough and went back to Denver.

By this time many months had passed, and many of my friends that were in the reformatory were now out of the reformatory. I remember one of the first things that happened was that I met some of those friends, and they said, "Come with us. We want you to meet a real cool fellow." I went with them, and we stepped up on a porch. One of the boys I was with had marijuana in his pocket. All of a sudden the police came up. We did not know they had been watching that house, but they drove up and ran up on the porch. This young fellow was able to throw the pot down on the porch with the leaves, and the police did not find it, but we were arrested for suspicion. That brought out everything—that I had broken out of the state reformatory, that I was in the army, and so on. They decided that they would send me back to the army and let the army deal with me first. After the army, I would have to go back and finish my time in the state reformatory, although I probably would go to another reformatory for older boys. I went in before a rough sergeant, and he asked me, "How many times have you been AWOL?" I told him I had never been AWOL and that I liked the army and had not been in any trouble. All of a sudden there was a sympathetic look in this sergeant's eye, and he wanted to help me. He began to investigate. Through searching documents he found that I went into the army too young, so he told me that if my mother would go to the Golden State Reformatory and secure a pardon for me from the reformatory, they would be able to give me a minority discharge, which is an honorable discharge. My mother went and pled for me at the state reformatory in Golden, Colorado. Since I had not been in any other trouble, they gave my mother a pardon for me. That pardon was sent to Fort Jackson in Columbia, South Carolina, and I was put out of the army with an honorable discharge.

I was free. I was free, I thought, at last. I thought that I had no more jail sentence to serve. I had even planned on going back and reenlisting in the Army Airborne, but I found I was enslaved to sin. I went from Columbia to Greenville where I had relatives. My dad at this time had moved back to Denver, Colorado, and I stayed with a cousin who was saved. She went to Tabernacle Baptist Church. She was a godly young lady who loved the Lord Jesus Christ. She lived for Him and walked with Him. She talked to me about the Lord. On one occasion she was hospitalized for surgery, and I went to the hospital to see her. In the hospital there were some men from Tabernacle Baptist Church. They opened a Bible, and for the very first time in my life I heard a clear presentation on how to be saved. They gave me a gospel tract. I doubled up that tract and put it in my billfold and carried it and read it and reread it several times. I was under deep conviction. People had started praying for me. At night I would feel like I was slipping into hell. I was afraid to die. I was afraid of hell. In those days they were talking about the atomic bomb ending the world. I was afraid the world would end and I would not be saved.

After my cousin got out of the hospital, she invited me one Sunday to eat with her and some friends. They came from church, and I went to her house. She had a friend, a beautiful young lady. She sat at the end of the table, and I could hardly take my eyes off of her. She felt so embarrassed—she was really trying to eat soup with a fork because she was so embarrassed, knowing I was looking at her. Then after we had eaten, I asked her if she would go someplace with me—any place. She said, "No, I am a Christian. I go absolutely nowhere with unsaved young men." Outwardly I felt like giving her a swift kick, but inwardly I respected a young lady who loved the Lord Jesus Christ more than anything else. Inwardly I had great admiration and respect. Then she said one word that gave hope to my heart. She said, "But if you were to go to church tonight, I would ask my mother if I could sit with you." I am not sure if she compromised right there or not, but I went to church that night. I did not go to hear preaching. I did not go to hear singing. I went to sit with that young lady. That was the only reason I went.

I heard Dr. Harold Sightler preach. He had his coat off and was screaming out, "You are a sinner." It seemed as if he were pointing right at me. I even moved the position I was in to the other part of the chair, but it still looked as if his finger were pointed right at me saying, "You are a sinner. You are a sinner." I knew that I was a sinner. I knew that if I died I was going to hell, but I walked out of that church that night unsaved. On a Monday night they had a tent meeting, and a lot of people from Tabernacle were there—especially a lot of the young people. I went to that meeting and saw the cleanliness of those young people. I saw the godliness of those young people, and in my heart I said, "I would like to be like they are." I sat near the front. I heard a man I have never seen since then—Homer Couch. I raised my hand for prayer. I did not know what to do, but I knew I needed the Lord. No one spoke to me. Had someone spoken to me, I would have gone forward and been saved right there in that tent meeting. I went home that night and opened the door of the house. I was still living with my cousin and my uncle and his family. I went through the front room and into the kitchen.

I did not turn on the light. The moon was gleaming on the window-panes, and I was walking back and forth. All of a sudden and once and for all I stopped and trusted the Lord Jesus Christ to save me. That night I was saved. What a difference! I never will forget trying to sleep that night. When my cousin came in, I told him that I had been saved and what a marvelous transformation had taken place in my life. I told him just exactly what had happened. I sat down and wrote my mother a long letter begging her to accept the Lord Jesus Christ. I wrote my dad begging him to accept the Lord Jesus Christ.

I was saved on Monday night. On Wednesday night I went to church and publicly gave a testimony. The minute I stepped on the grounds, young people came to me and asked me if I would like to go to the prayer room. When I was taken to the prayer room, there were so many people on their knees praying that I could hardly bow down. The fire of God was in my heart, and I wanted to do anything and everything for the Lord. Six months after I was saved, I went to my pastor and told him, "Dr. Sightler, I have been saved only a few months. I have read only as far as Isaiah, but I feel like God wants me to preach." He said, "Son, you have enough there to preach from now until eternity. Preach it." So I started preaching.

We preached all over the streets of Greenville. Some Saturdays we would preach nine times. Different men would preach. Some-times we had nine street meetings all over the city of Greenville. We preached in houses and in jails.

God is marvelous. He had given me wonderful friends—men and women who prayed and knew God and young people who loved God. It was a great blessing to me. The young lady who was instrumental in helping me come to be saved became my wonderful wife. She is the most gracious and loving wife in all the world. We have three children.

I do not know why it never dawned on me that I ought to get prepared to preach. I think some of the people in my home church thought I needed a lot of maturity before I was ready to go to Bible school. I became introduced to Bob Jones University through night classes. I remember the first time I was asked to pray in class. I was always used to just falling on my knees anywhere and everywhere, and I had not paid attention to how the others were praying. I just got out of my seat and fell down on my knees and started praying. When I got through I was embarrassed as I looked around and saw that everyone prayed while seated.

This same year Bob Jones University came out with a new program called the Institute of Christian Service. I had only gone through the ninth grade, but I was able to go into the Institute of Christian Service. What a blessing that was! I will never forget the teachers. Dr. Ken Hay was the director. How much time he put into the work! I remember how patiently he and many of the other teachers taught. It was a great time.

My feet had never been worthy even to step on that campus, but we were able to hear Dr. Bob Sr. I will never forget one Christmas as he was challenging us with the message that he would preach almost every Christmas: "The dog has gone back to his vomit, and the sow has gone back to her wallow." I could not help but think, "What if we go home and come back and dear Dr. Bob isn't here with us anymore?" As I walked out of the auditorium, I was weeping. We loved every one of our teachers. We loved Dr. Bob Jr. I appreciated everything that they did. I never did get to meet Dr. Bob Sr. personally or to talk with him. My wife had never met Dr. Bob Sr. until one day when she went to the campus to pay a bill. She had two of the children with her, and Dr. Bob walked up and starting talking to the children, and my wife was able to chat with him for a while. She said she felt so comfortable talking to such a learned man. It was just a blessing to know this, even though I personally was never able to talk to him. I had not personally talked to Dr. Bob Jr. until recently when he was here in Brazil. I never dreamed I would be able to meet and fellowship with him and Dr. Bob III. What a blessing each has been in my life—the sayings, the principles, the character that was instilled in us and driven down in us. I say "us" because it was put in me and then transmitted to my wife and to our children.

We finally came to our last year in the Institute of Christian Service. During the time we lived in Woodland Homes. Out in the woods I had a place where I would pray each morning before I went to school. I worked second shift. I would go in at four in the afternoon and get off at twelve at night. I would usually come home and do some work and study. I would get up early in the morning and go out to the woods to pray and have my Bible reading before I went to school. J. B. Williams was preaching at the missionary conference in our church. He gave a challenge to the young people to go anywhere that God wanted us to go. I will never forget the challenge. He did not ask us to go to Africa as a missionary. He asked for young people who would be willing to go *anywhere* that God wanted them to go. I imagine that about two hundred young people crowded down that aisle and bowed on their knees. At my side was my bosom buddy Bobby Powell. We were crying as we told God we were willing to go anywhere He wanted us to go. There were very few options as to mission boards. I will never forget the day we applied to BIMI, Baptist International Missions.

I am so grateful to three institutions that have meant so much to me, and I have never betrayed one of them. The first is my local church, Tabernacle Baptist Church, which I have stood by and honored, and not one time in my life have I criticized my pastor. The second is Bob Jones University, which has meant so much to me. The third is BIMI, the mission board I have been with—I think I may have been one of their first missionaries in 1961 when I applied.

In 1962 we were ready to go to Brazil. As we were flying across the ocean, I remember looking out and seeing the prop of one of the motors standing straight up, and fire was flashing out of the motor. The stewardess scared everyone to death by coming through and yelling, "Everyone fasten your seat belts," and she sat down and buckled her seat belt. The captain came on and said, "Ladies and gentlemen, we are going to have to make an unscheduled landing in Panama." Well, I was in favor of seeing the land again. We landed in Panama and got off the plane, and my wife said, "I will never get on an airplane again." I thought for a minute we were going to have to be missionaries to Panama instead of Brazil, but twenty-four hours later she got on exactly the same plane.

One of our next stops was Lima, Peru, where, in those days, they were having constant uprisings. In Lima she decided to get off the plane with some of the other ladies. She said she was going to get some chocolate candy. When she came to get back on the plane, there were armed guards blocking the exit that led out to the plane. They carried rifles with bayonets. The ladies tried to explain (none of them spoke Spanish) that this was their plane. The men just shook their heads and their fingers and spoke in Spanish. So they went and got the Braniff manager. He came down and tore into the guards with words, and there was arguing. Finally, he turned around and spoke to the ladies in English and said, "I am going to hit two of these men and knock them over. When I do, you ladies run to the airplane." He swung around and knocked two of the men down, and those ladies ran to the airplane. Needless to say, my wife did not want to get off the airplane after that!

We finally arrived in São Paulo, Brazil. I did not know one word of Portuguese, which is our language here in Brazil. I was scared to death, but I knew that God would take care of us. We went into the interior to a city called Batatais. We began looking for a storefront building we could rent. There were buildings available, but the minute we told them we were going to start a church and were the first Americans ever to live in that city, they would not give it to us. There was a little tiny Assembly of God church there that had twelve people in it. The preacher was from the city that I live in now, Ribeirao Preto. He was a humble seller of bananas. As he was selling bananas out on the street, a man tapped him on the shoulder; as the preacher turned around, the man shot him in the head—just because he was a preacher of the gospel. A priest tried to defend that man in court, but it so happened there was a circuit judge who was not a resident of Batatais, and he put all the priests out of the courtroom, and the man was sentenced. Of course, he stayed in jail only about three years.

We came to this kind of persecution. Because one preacher had been killed, everyone said it was a terrible place. Even the director of our mission board asked that I seriously consider going somewhere else and said that I might be able to start three or four churches somewhere else while I was trying to start one there, but we felt that Batatais was the place we should be. We went out to the large park where every Thursday and Saturday young people by the hundreds would walk around the park. That is how they met each other and dated, and we went there to preach. At our first street meeting we had a lady from São Paulo singing, and as she was singing, they began to throw giant firecrackers. The police had to be called to rescue us that night, but the gospel was preached. Many times I was run off from someone's house as we went door-to-door visiting. By the way, we visited every single house in that city (we estimated there were over five thousand houses because there were about thirty-five thousand people). We held street meetings, and God gave us some of the best Christians you could ever imagine. People began to get saved, but we did not have any place to meet, so we rented a tiny little garage. Having fifty people packed in that garage was misery. The heat was terrible, yet God blessed. We had seven preacher boys. Five of them are in the ministry right now in the city of Batatais.

We lived seven wonderful years in Batatais. Our young preachers were on fire for God. We witnessed to priests. We would stop them on the street. Another preacher boy and I even went into the main church and witnessed to the Monseigneur, which is the chief of all the priests. There were two priests' schools near Batatais. We went in and witnessed to them. We almost scared them to death, but we gave them the gospel. One young lady was saved her last year in a private school run by the nuns. She had to stick it out, and the persecution that was heaped upon her just made her more firm and more faithful.

In every church that we have started, God in mercy has raised up preachers, except the one in São Paulo where we were such a short time. After a church is established, it has been our policy here in Brazil to train a preacher out of the church. We have never taken another preacher from another church. It takes a little bit longer, but in each church we used our own preacher boy. In that church in Batatais, a preacher was ordained to the ministry.

We now labor in Ribeirao Preto. The reason we came to Ribeirao Preto was that we felt it was time for us to start a Bible institute. We had established churches in the area, and Ribeirao Preto would be the hub of a wheel. So we came and began to look for a storefront building. We first chose the biggest neighborhood that did not have a gospel witness in it. The upper part of Campos Eliseos at that time had a population of one hundred thousand people but had no Baptist church at all, so we were looking in that area. We had to leave the car and start walking the streets, and every time we saw someone working on a building we asked him if he knew of any place where there was a storefront building. I stopped one place, and the man said, "I am the owner. I am building this myself. I am about done." I asked him if he would rent it to us, and he said yes. We rented that place and started once again with just our family, and God began to move there and save people. We have been in this church nineteen years now. We founded Ebenezer Bible Institute and a camp, and now we are starting churches out of this church.

We also had another vision. It was a vision to teach the Brazilian churches to be missionary churches. God has blessed that. Here in this church right now our people promised to give the equivalent of $3,200 a month above their tithes in faith-promise giving. That is a lot of money for our people. We have some that make better and others that make just a minimum salary. But this church has caught the vision. We have been able to go back and implant faith-promise giving in the other churches, and in many churches around Brazil we have been able to preach missions. In the States and here in Brazil we have seen literally hundreds of young people come to the altar. I do not know how many are on mission fields today, but hundreds and hundreds have come and given their lives to go anywhere God wants them to go. Some are here in Brazil right now—Wade Dobson, Paul Pritchard. Those men surrendered to the mission field and came to Brazil. Many others are in various places of the world.

We hold revival meetings all over Brazil. There is not one evangelist in this country, so we have to go. All over Brazil from the north to the south to the east to the west we have traveled on buses, sometimes three days and three nights on dirt roads. We have slept sometimes in Sunday school rooms and on couches, but we are not complaining. Thank God for the many, many souls that have been saved.

14

Prayer and Provision

Prayer and Provision

AL BRADSHAW (ATTENDED 1953-57)

My folks sent me two dollars in my three and a half years at Bob Jones University. The very night that they told me, "Son, you are on your own," my systematic reading of the Bible brought me to Psalm 27:10: "When my father and my mother forsake me, then the Lord will take me up." I prayed, "OK, Lord, it is just You and me as we go to school."

I remember my first time in the broom closet at school. I got on my knees, and I said, "Lord, I need a dollar. I need just a dollar." You see, when I came to school, I had worked all summer in a steel company in Canada and saved every dime I could. I hitchhiked back and forth to work, which you could do in those days. I never bought a Coke; I never bought any goodies at the machine. I put every dime I had toward school, and when I came to school, I gave them everything I had; then I said, "How much do I have to work to pay the difference?" So they gave me a work-loan scholarship to pay the difference. The only thing is that I didn't have a dime of spending money—not a dime. Everything I got while I was at school I had to "pray in." I was able to pay my bill; I was able to work and make up the difference. But I had nothing for books, nothing for clothing, nothing for anything. The Snack Shop? I didn't know what that was until about my senior year. I didn't have any money to go to the Snack Shop. I want you to understand that when you get alone with God, God reaches down. So I was in the closet and telling God, "I need a dollar. You know I need a dollar because I have to get a book." As I got up, I opened the door, and there was a dollar underneath the door, and I said, "Lord, thank You." I was so excited.

The next time I went to the closet, I needed a dollar. (You are going to hear a lot about dollars.) By the way, that was a lot of money back then. Anyway, I had loaned a student a dollar, and I needed it, so I said, "Lord, I want You to remind Roy Shelpman that he owes me a dollar." I got out of the broom closet, went up to the third floor of the dormitory, and ran right into Roy. Roy said, "Al, remember you loaned me a dollar? Here it is." That will lift you up. That will cure homesickness.

The next time I got in the closet I said, "Lord, it is not so bad this time. I just need a stamp." To tell you when that was, I needed five cents for a stamp. I got out of the broom closet and walked toward the Alumni Building, and there was a nickel on the sidewalk. I said, "Thank You, Lord. That is exactly what I needed." I went and bought the stamp and put it on the letter and mailed it.

Every weekend we went on extension, and the last three years we went to Columbia. We had a servicemen's center. We went to a church pastored by Dr. Otis Holmes to do some children's work in the morning and to the servicemen's center all afternoon, and the last year I also worked on the University of South Carolina campus as Campus Crusade director. Every weekend it cost two dollars for extension—one dollar was to buy gas for the GI who drove the car (GIs were the only ones who had cars back then), and the other dollar was for the noon meal at a boarding house where we could get all we could eat for a dollar. (You can imagine how long ago it was!) So every week I would have to say, "Lord, I want to go on extension; You know I want to go. If You want me to go, You are going to have to take care of me." You say, "That is kind of familiar, isn't it?" He is my Father. I am not being light about it, but I have come to know Him, and I praise Him for who He is and for His holiness and His majesty; but I praise Him that He is personal. When they said, "Lord, teach us to pray," Jesus said, "When you pray, say 'Our Father.' " I don't have a father. I don't have a father-in-law now, but I have a heavenly Father, and He is the same yesterday, today, and forever.

One weekend I had no dollars—I had nothing. It would have been so easy to say, "Well, I am going to stay home." But I got in the car and said, "Lord, You know I don't even have the dollar for gas." We pulled up to a gas station, and a faculty member walked over and said, "You boys going to Columbia?" We said, "Yes." He said, "I will pay your gas if you will give me a ride down." I said, "Get in." I wasn't even driving!

So I got down there, and I was so happy God got me down there. Then we went visiting, and this time I was doing the athletic dorm at the University of South Carolina and was over there by myself. I looked at my watch and said, "It is twelve o'clock, and I don't have any money." I said, "Lord, I'm hungry," but nothing happened. I stood looking out a window, and I was praying. Honestly, I wasn't the type that cried then, but some tears were going down because I felt sorry for myself. I was hungry, and I said, "Lord, I have been to every room in this dormitory. I have knocked at every door, and nobody is at home. They are all eating. It's twelve, and I don't have anything to eat." He said, "Keep knocking." I went to the next door and knocked, and a guy said, "Come in." I was shocked. I walked in and said, "I am Al Bradshaw with Campus Crusade for Christ, and I would like to take a survey if you have a minute." He said, "You won't believe it, but I would like you to take that. This is the only time I have been on the campus on the weekend. I always go home on Friday night, but I had a paper to do. I just finished, and I have time." So I took the survey with him and finished with the question, "If you died today, do you know where you would spend eternity?" He looked at me and said, "I sure don't, but I sure would like to know," and I led him to the Lord. You see, if I had had money, I wouldn't have ever reached that young man for Christ.

In the afternoon I was still knocking on doors. I knocked at one, and the fellow said, "Come in." When I walked in, there was a guy with two bushels of beautiful North Carolina apples, and I said, "Where did you get those apples?" He said, "My father grows them. Would you want one?" I thought he would never ask. I got two, and they were the best apples I had ever eaten, and that was my meal. I thanked the Lord all day for those two apples because at the servicemen's center that night we could eat.

The next week I went on extension again. This time I had a dollar. I gave it for the gas. When we got down to Columbia, I did my work on the college campus and met the guys at noon where we always met. We just got to talking and walking along, and before I knew it, we were heading in to eat. I said, "Oh-oh, I don't have any money." The Lord said, "Go on in and eat." Now, He didn't talk out loud (and please don't do this), but I went into the restaurant with no money. When we prayed, I silently said, "Lord, help, I need a dollar." I was halfway through the meal and enjoying it when a guy tapped me on the shoulder and said, "You remember me?" I said, "Yes, I saw you in the dorm." He said, "I gave you two apples." I said, "Oh yes, sure." He said, "I want you to know I just paid for your meal." I took out my wallet and said, "I want to show you something." It was bare, and I said, "You will never know what you just did—how that encouraged my heart." He was a Christian.

When it came time to graduate, I needed sixty-nine dollars to graduate, and I couldn't take my exams until I paid. I had ten dollars and went to the mailbox. My sister had sent me fifty dollars from Canada, so now I had sixty dollars. I went to the post office that evening and said, "Well, maybe . . ." There was a five-dollar bill from California. There was no note, just a five-dollar bill in an envelope postmarked from California. So I said, "Sixty-five dollars!" I was walking my fiancée Lu Ann home. We had an agreement that she would pray for me but would never tell anyone nor would she ever in any way give me money. She never had financial troubles. She had physical troubles and had to drop out a year because of surgery. I had no physical troubles but had financial troubles. So we had this agreement. I said, "Lu Ann, pray for me tonight. I need four dollars in the morning in order to take my exams." I no sooner said that than Jim McCoy from Iowa tapped me on the shoulder and said, "Hey, Al, remember that first semester you sold me a book? Here are the four dollars I owe you." I said, "Hallelujah!" Lu Ann stared at me with a look that said, "Wow!"

She saw this in action after she married me. One night we didn't have a thing. She said, "Honey, there is nothing to eat, and I went out and gathered some pop bottles so we have enough milk for the baby. But we don't have a thing for the morning." "What are *we* going to have?" I said. "Let's pray right now, Lu Ann." So we got on our knees in front of the couch in Houston, Texas, and I said, "Lord, You have met our needs. You always have. Our checks haven't come in, and we have no food. Lord, we are dependent upon You to meet our needs." We got up, and I wiped her tears away.

About that time there was a knock on the door. She dashed to the bedroom to fix up, and I went to the front door. There were a millionaire and his wife who were our sponsors for the Campus Crusade at the University of Houston and Rice, and they were standing there with two big bags. I said, "Mr. Hogan, come on in." He said, "Well, Dot and I were out driving, and we said, 'Let's drop in and see how Al and Lu are doing,' and Dot said, 'Let's stop and pick up some groceries.'" He put them down on our table, and being the type of man he was, he opened the refrigerator to help me put them away. He said, "There is nothing in there but a bottle of water! What were you going to have for breakfast?" I said, "Those things in the bags." He said, "Al, you don't understand. You have to eat. You can't do that!" I said, "Mr. Hogan, my wife and I just got off our knees, and when we got up off our knees, the knock came at the door. We had prayed for someone to bring us food, and you just walked in." He said, "I'll fix that." He picked up the phone and called his secretary at home and said, "Gwen, this is Hogan. I just want you to know that if Al and Lu ever have need of money, whatever they need, you give it to them. Have you got that straight? They will pay you back, but you give it to them." He said, "There, you will never have to want again." I said, "Mr. Hogan I have a better deal than that. I have a heavenly Father who, when I ask Him, sends it in, and I don't have to give it back."

We left Campus Crusade that same year. We had had a wonderful ministry at the University of Houston and Rice—almost two hundred people coming to know the Lord. It was thrilling to win souls and bring them in and train them. When we started, I didn't know anyone, and we had a high of ninety-two students in our house one night. But we had to leave Campus Crusade because the director no longer stood where he used to stand when he stood in the pulpit at BJU. He promised that he had the same philosophy of evangelism as Bob Jones did, but there he was in Mound, Minnesota, now saying, "I will sit with Billy Graham at the Cow Palace [San Francisco] or any other place he wants me to sit; nobody is going to tell me where to sit or where to pray." I said, "Bill, you promised us." He said, "Dr. Bob Jones Sr. is a blackmailer, and you are afraid not to follow him." I said, "Dr. Bob Jones is a man of

God, and he has taught me most of what I know, and as far as my wife and I are concerned, we're gone." We got up and walked out of that place. That whole room there in Mound, Minnesota, was full of Bob Jones graduates. I couldn't believe it; only three of us left at that time. Lu and I had a two-month-old baby, and Lu said, "Where are we going?" I said, "I don't know. Let's run by and see Mom and Dad. I will leave you with them and then go down to see Dr. Bob Sr." So I came down to talk with him.

I ended up teaching in a public school in Man, West Virginia. I taught U.S. history second semester, and I had had only one semester of U.S. history and am a Canadian! Mr. Hogan called us and said, "Al, come to Texas, and we will start a youth ranch." We went there for two years, but I knew this was not what God wanted me to do. I said, "Mr. Hogan, I am not happy about trying to start a ranch. God doesn't want me to do that." He said, "Al, I want to talk to you. I want you to know I am worth thirty million in Dun & Bradstreet. I am Houston's best builder. If you will leave the ministry and come with me and take my son's place" (who had died of cancer, and through that Mr. Hogan and his wife got saved), "I will leave all the money to you to invest and use as you see fit." I said, "Mr. Hogan—" He said, "Don't give me an answer now. I will give you thirty days."

I came here and saw Dr. Bob Sr. I said, "Dr. Bob, if I get that thirty million, I could give Bob Jones a million, and this one a million. . . . You know me; I am not going to make any headlines." He said, "Al, you have to do what *God* wants you to do." On the way home in the car (that was my closet), I said, "Lord, what do *You* want me to do?" The verse came to me, "For the gifts and calling of God are without repentance" (Rom. 11:29). God doesn't change His mind. Then He said, "Woe is unto me, if I preach not the gospel" (I Cor. 9:16). I walked into Mr. Hogan's office, and I said, "Mr. Hogan, I am sorry, but I have to preach." He said, "You are a fool." I said, "Then I will be a fool for Jesus' sake. I have got to preach."

He said, "What are you going to do? You don't have a job; you have nothing. You have your wife and baby—what are you going to do?" I said, "Well, I am just going to get a job until the Lord opens the door. I know that God is calling me to be a pastor, which I had vowed I would never be." He said, "Well, I have a dump truck out there; I will put you to work." So I drove the dump truck.

Picking up trash is a tough job. One day I was picking up trash after a small hurricane came through Houston. I was at the back of the truck picking up things, and the water was up to my knees, over the top of my boots. The other two guys who were supposed to help me were sitting on the front bumper taking a break, and I had all I could take. I will never forget. I looked up to heaven and said, "God, I don't understand. I am a Bob Jones graduate. I have served You, and I want to serve You. I just don't understand, Lord." God didn't speak to me in words, but in my heart He said, "If I ever bless you, remember where I found you."

A couple of weeks later I took my first pastorate in Eatonton, Georgia, and God blessed there and worked in a wonderful way. We took a tiny church and built a new one, built a parsonage, and left them with about 150 people. We pulled them out of the convention (don't ever do that unless you are close to the Lord) and left them as an independent Baptist church that is still there today.

We went to Tampa, Florida; that church had been sued by another church. I didn't know that. After one month of being there, I knew I had made a terrible mistake. I got on my knees and said, "God, if You will get me out of here, I will go right back to Georgia. I will apologize to those people. I will be their pastor until the cows come home. I can't take this. But if You want me here, Lord, give me something." This is in the closet now. That day, systematically reading my Bible, I was in I Thessalonians 5, and there are a lot of good verses there; but finally I came to verse 24: "Faithful is he that calleth you, who also will do it." I said, "Lord, if You have called me, then You do it. It is Yours. I give You Hillsdale Baptist Church. If it falls apart, it is Your fault. If it becomes a great church, it is to Your glory. But it is Your church; I give it to You. And I promise You this, I will never seek to leave. If You want me to leave Hillsdale, You come after me." By the grace of God we have been there twenty-nine years. We have seen it grow. We have seen the number of our missionaries grow. We give $140,000 a year to missions; and every time we put up a new building (and all of our buildings are debt-free), I don't see the building. I see the dump truck, and I say, "Lord, thank You for the dump truck. It is a great thing to show me who I am and where I would be except by Your grace."

The Lord called Dr. Al Bradshaw home to heaven in August 1995.

15

College Recruiter in Guadalcanal

College Recruiter in Guadalcanal

RAY SEAY (ATTENDED 1946-51)

I was the youngest of nine children. My parents, who were very poor and lived in the country, died when I was only nineteen months old. Seven of my brothers and sisters and I were sent to a Methodist children's home in central Florida. The year was 1922.

When I was five years old, my oldest sister and her husband, a Methodist minister, adopted me. He died, however, when I was fourteen. I called my sister "mother" until I was seventeen.

In 1940 I joined the U.S. Marine Corps. Four of my brothers also joined the military. Soon after joining the marines, I was ordered to Iwo Jima. We arrived there during the night of February 18, 1945. I was with the Fourth Marine Division, Third Battalion, I Company, 25th Marines.

For the next five days I was ordered to stay aboard ship. Our division suffered heavy losses. I was then told to take ammunition and gasoline ashore with another soldier. From Tuesday through Saturday we did this. On one of those days we came under heavy machine-gun fire from a Japanese ship. My friend was wounded, and he was rushed to a hospital ship. Not long afterward a kamikaze pilot flew his plane into the ship, and my friend was killed.

On Sunday morning, February 26, I was going ashore at Iwo Jima. A bullet hit the thick strap on my backpack and stopped before penetrating my body. I was then ordered to carry a flamethrower on my back, even though I had no training in how to operate one. As I was walking up a hill with other marines, gunfire suddenly erupted, and my lieutenant was killed right in front of me. I quickly pulled the flamethrower off my back and threw it over the side of a cliff. I knew that if a tracer bullet hit it, I would be blown to pieces.

For the rest of the morning, we were pinned down in foxholes and could not move. A soldier carrying a message to another platoon suddenly stopped beside my foxhole. A bullet struck him. I pulled him into the hole, bandaged his wound and gave him morphine. After that he began to talk to me. He asked me if I were a Christian, and I told him I was a church member. After talking to the soldier for a few minutes, I learned an amazing thing. He lived right across from the orphanage where I had lived in central Florida. I then pulled a letter from his pack and read it to him. It was from his mother. She wrote that she hoped he was trusting the Lord. Later that day, the gunfire stopped . . . but it was too late. By sundown, the young man was dead.

The next morning I was standing with some other marines. We were talking and joking as our sergeant lit up a cigarette. In a matter of seconds, a Japanese mortar shell landed right in the middle of us. My sergeant and four other soldiers were killed, and I was knocked down. Another sergeant standing nearby went berserk and pulled out his pistol. He looked as if he were going to shoot me, but a lieutenant standing nearby tackled him and held him to the ground until other soldiers arrived.

Later that afternoon, God began dealing with me as I stood looking over the Pacific Ocean. I told Him if He would spare my life and get me back to the States, I would serve Him. Later I returned to the battlefield and found myself in a foxhole with three other soldiers for a couple of days. One was a Baptist preacher's son and one was an atheist, but he loved to hear the Baptist preacher's son read from a Gideon Bible.

Before long a soldier from West Virginia moved into our infantry. He had a riot gun, a ten-gauge shotgun that he called "Barkin' Betsy." He told me he would like to get off this "hellhole." Jokingly, I told him just to stand up. He did and was immediately hit in the neck by a sniper's bullet. But it was only a surface wound, and he sat back down in the foxhole and began to laugh hysterically. I put a bandage on the man's wound and asked him if he were hurt. He said he was feeling fine because he would get to spend time on a hospital ship with good-looking nurses. He then took his gun off his shoulder and handed it to me. He said he would not need it any longer. I kept the gun during the remainder of my stay on Iwo Jima and then mailed it home.

On the day I left Iwo Jima, I saw thousands of crosses. Each one marked the grave of an American soldier. At that point, God began dealing with me again. I remembered a song that I sang as a little boy in a choir in Florida: "The Old Rugged Cross." That evening while returning home aboard a ship, I was given a huge steak with all the trimmings, but I could eat only three bites.

Days later I arrived in Maui, but I was all alone. Two of my buddies were dead, and the other was severely wounded. I went into a deep depression and began drinking heavily. I got really messed up. The war seemed so senseless. Later that day the headlines in the *Honolulu Advertiser* declared "A-Bomb Dropped on Japan." Although I was sad that thousands had been killed by the bomb, I rejoiced that the war would soon be over.

I returned to the States in October 1945 but re-enlisted in the marines. Following my second stint in the marines, I found myself on a street corner in Los Angeles. I had been drinking and was walking to a bus station. I was going home. But a man from the Salvation Army walked over and handed me a gospel tract. I told him to mind his own business. His response stunned me. He said, "This *is* my business. You take it." I read the tract on the bus that evening, and the Holy Spirit began to convict me.

After arriving home, I began thinking about entering Bob Jones University in Cleveland, Tennessee. A corporal I had met briefly on Guadalcanal during the war had talked to me about Jesus Christ and told me about the school. A couple of days after speaking with the man, I had returned to see him again but was told that he was dead. He had been hit by a bomb on the very spot where he told me about the Lord's saving grace. With the words of that young man still burning within me, I enrolled at Bob Jones University. On Easter Sunday during my freshman year, I heard Dr. Bob Jones, founder of the school, preach on heaven. After the service, I went back to my room and accepted Christ as my Lord and Savior.

Eventually I graduated from the University and became a minister of the gospel. In 1950 I began pastoring my first church. Since that time I have organized ten churches and pastored five churches in five states. In 1991 I retired as pastor of Welcome Valley Baptist Church. Since then my wife, Margaret, and I have been involved in a ministry at a local correctional institution. I am also involved in evangelism. Everywhere I go, I give people gospel tracts and tell them about Jesus.

16

Daddy Short Legs

Daddy Short Legs
PETER MARUYAMA (ATTENDED 1961-63)

When I was a small boy I read a story called *Daddy Long Legs*. This book tells about a girl whose education is paid for by a man she doesn't know, whom she refers to as "Daddy Long Legs." Can such a thing happen in a man's life? Is it just a story?

I was born in Japan in 1932 as the eleventh child of a Buddhist family. My father lost his parents when he was a small boy and was raised by a Buddhist priest. It was not strange that he gave the children very strict discipline. The children were told to do good works to go to Paradise. I was shy, timid, and depressive. I was not good at communicating myself to others. My brother often teased me that I had such a long tongue that my Japanese pronunciation could hardly be understood. He suggested that I should eat lots of potatoes and butter and learn to speak English! That I did, although we did not have enough food to eat right after World War II.

In February 1947 a unique English radio broadcast began over the NHK network (the only broadcast over Japan then). By the recommendation of the GHQ, a non-English teacher, Mr. Joe T. Hirakawa, started a fifteen-minute conversation program. He was the English announcer of the NHK overseas broadcast who read the emperor's message of surrender. In his program he used a very familiar children's song as the theme song, changing the words: "Come, come, everybody!" He had studied at Washington University, majoring in drama before the war, so his pronunciation and elocution were excellent. The whole country was gloomy after the war and people had little food, no hope, and no entertainment at all. This English radio program caught the attention of millions of the Japanese. He soon became one of the most well-liked persons in the country. My parents and I were staying in Nagano, a small country village, which was about 180 km from Tokyo. We had left

Tokyo after the big bombing of B-29s in 1945. Village children were not kind to the "intruders." They often threw stones at me.

Just about that time I heard the Come Come English over the radio. I listened to it every day and enjoyed practicing English conversation with my pals as the lecturer suggested. Soon I had gathered many friends around this broadcast. Mr. Hirakawa said over the radio every month not to give up our English play. He never said anything about study. He said that his method was God-given. As a baby learns his mother's tongue, all we have do is just imitate the mother and play speaking! By *mother,* he meant the lecturer or an American. We saw many U.S. soldiers around us; one time, I gathered the courage to speak to one of them on the train.

My family came back to Tokyo in 1949. I started a Come Come Club in our city and also at my high school. I was able to rent a room in a police station in our town free of charge. Soon we had more than 120 members joining our English circle. We had meetings twice a week. The interpreter of that police station joined us also. We often had short visits from MPs, and we all enjoyed speaking broken English! There was laughter and great enthusiasm of mimicry. Big newspapers, including the *Asahi, Yomiuri,* and *Mainichi* all reported our activities in their local columns at various times. I invited many of the similar clubs to hold a nationwide gathering of English fans in Tokyo. Thus a timid boy had a chance to meet the lecturer in person. Hearing about my zeal, Mr. Hirakawa invited me to work for him. My father used to tell me, "Son, do not become a Christian." When he found out that I was going to an English Bible class, he told me, "Son, do not be a Christian minister. There are so few Christians in Japan, and you will not be able to support your life!" Getting close to Mr. Hirakawa, I was greatly impressed to see him pray before his preparation for the broadcast. He always wrote every word of his program, timing it and practicing intonation. He spent many hours preparing fifteen-minute broadcasts. I worked for him as his assistant, substitute teacher for small classes, editor of his textbook, and private teacher for his four children. His personal life encouraged me to study the Bible. Later I was told that he had been an assistant pastor of a church in America years ago.

The great enthusiasm for English study was introduced in America through big newspapers and soon we were surprised to receive more than fifteen hundred letters from American young people requesting pen pals. It was my duty to give those letters to hundreds of Japanese people, young and old, who were eager to correspond with Americans. The Come Come English created a pro-America atmosphere among the Japanese. After sending the letters to the fans, I saw one postcard left from an eight-year-old girl. No Japanese student wanted to correspond with such a small girl, so I took the time to help her know more of our country. After a few correspondences, the girl got tired of writing. Then her mother took up the correspondence, with whom we are still keeping contact. Years passed. I dedicated my life to the Lord and studied at Japan Baptist Bible College. After graduating, I had a burden to take the gospel to the Chinese.

As the first step I tried to get in contact with a missionary in Taiwan. There was no response. Several missionaries told me about Moody Bible Institute. That was about the only name we heard so often from American missionaries. In one of my letters I wrote to Mrs. Kraning about my desire to go to the States to apply for a scholarship at Moody. She wrote me back immediately and said, "I have been showing your letters to my father, Mr. Daniel Speicher. He has helped some young people in Asia. He is quite interested in you and wants to help you." Mr. Speicher, ninety-two years old then, wrote to me afterwards. "I would like to help you pay half of the tuition. I have given some donations to Bob Jones University. If you are willing to study at BJU, let me know about it." I wrote him back with thanks, "My wife and I really desire to follow the Lord all our ways, but there is no way for us to pay for the transportation, neither to pay half of the tuition. As servants of God, we do not desire to owe any debt to anybody." The correspondence stopped over a period of three months or more. In November 1960 a very thick envelope arrived from Mr. Speicher. There were three checks—one for the boat, one for textbooks, and one for my spending money at school. "Peter, I have paid your tuition at BJU. Are you willing to apply for a work-loan scholarship? Come for the second semester." Further he said, "This is not from me, but from the Lord. You owe me nothing." My wife was four months pregnant. We decided to accept the offer and praised the Lord. I left Yokohama port crying and praising the Lord on New Year's Eve.

Mr. Speicher was a small gentleman, smaller than a Japanese. He had lost one of his eyes and had a glass eye. He had a company of about one hundred workers. The Cyclone Seed Sower was his business. His wife had prayed much daily for the Japanese to be saved. They had given a church building to the Lord. Mrs. Speicher had a smaller prayer room in the chapel. She spent many hours praying for lost souls, I heard.

After two blessed years at BJU, I came back to Japan and started Narashino Baptist Church. We started our work without any support. About the middle of the night in the winter of 1965, we were surprised to see an old American lady knocking at our door. She had a piece of paper on which was written my name and a simple address: Makuhari, Chiba, Japan. She looked for our house with no indication of the street or number! "Are you Peter?" the lady asked. "I am Mrs. Myriam Faust. My father is Mr. Daniel Speicher. How wonderful to see you in Japan!"

The Lord has a purpose in everyone's life. The Daddy Long Legs in my case was a Daddy Short Legs. How could I ever betray my God who is so faithful in keeping His promises?